If Wine Could Talk

KARA JOSEPH

Indigo River Publishing

Indigo River Publishing
3 West Garden Street, Ste. 718
Pensacola, FL 32502
www.indigoriverpublishing.com

If Wine Could Talk | Kara Joseph, author
ISBN 978-1-950906-94-9 | LCCN 2021900369

Edited by Tanner Chau and Regina Cornell
Cover design by James Chakhtoura
Interior design by Robin Vuchnich

Special discounts are available on quantity purchases by corporations, associations, and others.

For details, contact the publisher at the address above.
Orders by US trade bookstores and wholesalers: please contact the publisher at the address above.

With Indigo River Publishing, you can always expect great books, strong voices, and meaningful messages. Most importantly, you'll always find . . . words worth reading.

For my parents, Terri and Brad, who inspired my love of people and wine. They taught me to truly see others, to share wine's magic, and to make life a grand adventure.

Contents

Introduction

WINE ALWAYS HAD A WAY OF SPEAKING TO ME, even if I didn't quite understand what it was saying. Upon making a decision to spend my life pursuing wine, I began to hear it loud and clear. I knew it had to be more than a rich man's drink, a lifestyle trend, or just frivolous alcohol. I resolved it had a deeper meaning. In the years of trying to understand wine's whole story, it ended up crafting mine.

If Wine Could Talk is the intertwining of two personal stories, one about wine and one about myself. My goal is to tell wine's story in tandem with my own. In this way, I can give wine the authentic voice it deserves. I want you to learn about wine as I learned, little by little. Each *Wine Talk* section seeks to answer the most common questions and misconceptions I've encountered in teaching wine throughout the years. You will gain a foundation of wine knowledge to build upon for years to come. More importantly, you can use wine to create your own story. That's when wine comes full circle and why I live for it.

1

Why Wine?

EVERYONE HAS A STORY TO TELL, and wine happens to be mine. All "wine people" tend to have their romanticized tale of how it took hold of their lives. Most of them tell a glamorous story about the moment they decided it was their true passion. Sometimes you hear the one about them growing up with wine, or the one about the legendary bottle they tasted, or the one about traveling to exotic lands to taste the finest juice. Perhaps it would serve me well to have a regal account as to why wine matters so much to me.

I can't lie and say I knew it was special from my first sip, or during family trips to France, or by drinking iconic wines growing up. My wine origins were authentic and from a place of unexpected love. My passion for wine wasn't a huge epiphany, for that matter. It started as simply something that made me happy. The happiness it brought me turned into something more meaningful. My parents were responsible for this. They were the ones to ignite the embers inside me.

Like it or not, our parents have a deep effect on us. They provide the very basis for who we will be. They provide the lens through which we view the world. The part of my upbringing I admire most was my parents having us sit down to dinner together every night. Nowadays, families rarely have time to be together, let alone share a meal. I can still remember more laughs, stories, and warmth around our dinner table than anywhere else in the world. Even today, I would choose to be sitting around my family's dining room table over visiting the most enchanting places in the world. I learned what was most important in life at our table. It seems almost fitting that was where I discovered my love of wine.

However, wine never had a profound presence in my parents' lives while I was growing up. The earliest wine memories I have are of my mom always ordering Cabernet Sauvignon for family dinners out. Every time, without fail. My parents weren't exactly what you would call *wine connoisseurs* during my childhood. They just weren't in the epicenter of fine wine culture in Jacksonville, Florida. When I entered college, their eyes were about to be opened to a whole new wine world. They were able to travel more once their nest was completely empty. Their most adventurous trip up to that point had been to somewhere like the mountains of Tennessee. They finally made their way to California and Napa Valley. I thought it was an odd choice for my parents, but they took off for the West Coast.

My dad texted me pictures of all the beauty they experienced throughout the two weeks of their visit. I thought it all looked like something out of a dream. Upon their return, something was different about my mom and dad. Something had rubbed off on them during those two weeks in wine country. It seemed insane, but my parents lit up in a way I hadn't ever seen before when they would talk about their California adventure. The stories were full of sights, tastes, and wines. I loved every chance I had to soak up each story and feel some of the wonder they felt.

After their whirlwind trip wine graced our table more than ever before. It was as though the wine took my parents back to who they had been in Napa—full of life. I can still see my mom and dad opening a bottle of Rombauer Chardonnay and twirling it around in their glasses. Closing their eyes, they would smell and taste the wine. It seemed as if this drink was bringing all the memories back.

As I watched this transformation in my parents, wine started looking differently to me. Wine wasn't just booze anymore. In a way I didn't quite understand yet, it could transport people back to a time, a place, or an emotion.

During this Joseph family wine renaissance, I was a sophomore at the University of Florida. The only wine I experienced was on Penny Wine Nights at a local wing joint. The trashy spot would pack the place by charging a penny for a mini plastic cup of the cheapest wine they could find. It was my idea of a refined night out. Penny

Wine Night consequently could've spelled disaster for my future in wine. I experienced my first real hangover (I thought I was hit by a car the next morning) after spending about twenty-five cents one night. You can do the math on that one. Franzia was a staple, and cooking wine comprised the majority of my wine consumption. I certainly didn't care much about what filled my plastic cup at that point. Everyone has to start somewhere with wine. I started at the absolute bottom.

On trips home to visit my parents, I escaped the college garbage. In my eyes, I was experiencing the upper crust of wine with them. They had real glasses, the wine they poured didn't come out of a box, and they actually talked about the stuff instead of just slugging it back. My parents would give me little sips during my underage days. The baby tastes of California Chardonnay were my way into wine culture. Sitting around the table with my parents sharing wine brought me so much joy. In this small way, my parents cracked the door to the world of wine to me, ultimately shaping my future.

Honestly, I just loved being with my parents. They could have been talking about changing the oil in a car and I would have hung on every word. Seeing their eyes light up when they spoke of wine, I began to cherish this beverage, which was so meaningful to them. Every wine we sipped had something more behind it than just being a delicious liquid. Every new bottle brought stories of the vineyards they'd visited, how the wine was made, and how to taste it. We weren't drinking the most elegant wine, and my parents weren't experts, but those details didn't matter. I fell in love with sharing moments together over wine. Every taste evoked a sense of fascination within me.

After returning to college, no more boxed wine for me. I had graduated to at least ten-dollar bottles (because I was now an expert). In my mind, I had legitimate knowledge. I became the "wine girl" among my friends. I was always the first to host wine nights. My joie de vivre with wine was unstoppable. I would suggest a wine bar near campus so I could share all my wine prowess with fellow sophistication seekers. As I did this, I saw the same light in my friends' eyes as I'd had when I first began to appreciate it. I started to view this beverage as my way to affect people. I can still see the looks of intrigue on their faces when I would recite the five *S*s of wine tasting my parents had taught me. Granted, I knew nothing about what I was actually saying. I would tell everyone to see, swirl, smell, sip, and, most importantly, savor the wine. These words became my tagline, and I must have proudly repeated them nearly a hundred times.

So that was it—I had fallen in love with wine. The romance didn't begin with knowing the science of wine, the iconic producers, how to make money off it, or even what a sommelier was. My passion started as a way to connect to the people around me, whether it be my parents connecting with me or me connecting with my friends. Wine fascinated me and made me want to know more about what made it so special.

Wine Talk: The Basics

Teaching the basics of wine always takes me back to one of my first experiences sharing my passion. One particular moment that stands out was my Walt Disney World–themed college graduation costume party. Everyone flocked to my apartment decked out in elaborate character outfits. I dressed as Walt Disney himself, complete with his signature mustache.

At this festive send-off, I took every chance I could to share the small pieces of wine knowledge I had acquired with my friends. It might have been because Snow White, Peter Pan, Jasmine, Olaf, and several other characters were staring back at me, but there was something magical about teaching wine to those around me.

My Disney wine event remains a subtle reminder of how to teach the wine basics: be approachable, easy to understand, and inspiring, just like your favorite Disney character.

What Is Wine?

Wine is merely the juice of grapes fermented into an alcoholic beverage. A lot of people think wine has to be more than that because of the array of flavors and aromas. They believe that winemakers have to add other fruits or flavorings. The aromas, flavors, and structure primarily come from the genetic makeup of the grape and the chemical change that occurs during fermentation. We can go a lot deeper, but knowing this simple fact is the best place to start.

When this realization hit me, grapes took on an otherworldly identity in my mind. The wonder of wine is that it can be endlessly complicated, debated, studied, and obsessed over, but in the end, it's fermented grape juice. And that's the beauty of it.

What are the main grapes I should know, and what makes them different?

The following are the primary grapes you may want to know to give you a sturdy foundation of wine knowledge: Chardonnay, Pinot Grigio, Sauvignon Blanc, Riesling, Pinot Noir, Cabernet Sauvignon, Syrah, and Merlot. These are all popular and, at times, misunderstood grapes. Basic knowledge of these major grapes will give you a solid base to build upon or at least help you navigate a wine list.

Chardonnay is a white grape variety that is considered an "international" grape variety because it is planted in almost every area where viticulture is possible. The style of wine Chardonnay produces will most likely have a medium weight on the palate and notes of fresh and ripe tropical fruits, and it will often have seen oak usage. Though there are various styles of this grape, depending on where the vines are grown, you can look to Chardonnay if you want a wine with good weight on the palate, intensity of flavor, and ease of pairing with many different foods. Some skeptics think they have Chardonnay nailed down, but try some from around the world and give this grape a chance for rediscovery.

Pinot Grigio is a white grape variety that is misunderstood and misrepresented. A lot of people see this grape as bland and tasteless. However, it can produce interesting and complex wines. In general, the wine we know best and love is our Italian Pinot Grigio. The better-quality Italian Pinot Grigios have a subtle apple and citrus presence and a touch of yeastiness, with a crushed rock minerality running through them. This grape can also be called Pinot Gris. Don't let this confuse you. It's the same grape just called by another name. Think of it like some people saying "soda" versus "pop." Pinot Gris is found mainly in Oregon and a place in France called Alsace.

Oregon Pinot Gris have an aromatic apple/pear character, slightly more heaviness on the palate, and less crisp acid than a Pinot Grigio. Pinot Gris from Alsace can be the most unique expression of this grape. The style of wine here can have added richness, more spiciness on the nose, and even more layers of flavor when you taste it. You can go for this grape when you want something crisp and refreshing from Italy or when you want something more complex and layered (lots of flavors hitting your palate at different times) from Alsace.

Sauvignon Blanc is a white grape variety that generally produces racy and crisp wines. The big thing to remember about this "cougar juice" (as one old coworker would call it) is that it will give off citrus-fruit aromas and flavors. There can be an evident green/herbaceous quality in the wine and mouthwatering acid as well. Overall, Sauvignon Blancs have a lighter color, more intense smells, higher acid, and a lighter body. This is always a sharp and sassy wine.

Riesling is the one grape I never thought I would respect. Grandmas always ordered it, so it blew my mind when I began trying quality Rieslings from Germany, New York State, and France. This white wine wasn't just a sugary-sweet wine, but rather a wine that had character and balance. What I mean by this is that the wines can have a sharp and electric acid that makes your mouth water and then a background of richness with a bit of residual sugar. Riesling is typically on the lighter-bodied side, with aromatic notes of stone fruit and honeysuckle flowers creating a flavorful, bright wine taste. Rieslings are beautiful food-pairing wines and can benefit from extended aging.

Pinot Noir is considered the chameleon of red grapes. This is because Pinot Noir can change dramatically in style depending on where in the world it is grown and how the wine is made. The main thing I want to get across here is that Pinot Noir can make wines that are the finest of the finest or the worst of the worst. Pinot Noir is thin-skinned and challenging to grow. The main character of the resulting wine is lighter in color and concentration. The wine will have primarily red fruits, spices, herbs, and a smoky cedar toast if the wine sees some new oak. Go for a Pinot Noir when you want that easy-breezy drinking feeling. When made right, you can get that feeling with a thought-provoking side to boot.

Cabernet Sauvignon is another of those key international grape varieties, much like Chardonnay. Cabernet Sauvignon has historically been considered the grape "serious" red wine drinkers enjoy. But there is more to this grape than just a strong flavor profile and recognizable character. People say you can grow it darn near anywhere, and it won't have the huge swings of flavor and quality like Pinot Noir does. I believe its consistent style is why people gravitate toward this grape. With most Cabernet Sauvignon you can look forward to a darker and brooding kind of wine. Blackberry, dark cherry, anise, tobacco, and more vanilla from oak can be seen on the nose and palate from this wine. When you enjoy a Cabernet Sauvignon, you can expect fuller body and more drying grip of the tannin. Cabernet Sauvignon can hold its own against a wide range of rich foods, so next decadent meal, pop open a bottle.

Syrah/Shiraz is one of my favorite red wine grapes in the world. I can have this grape from the Rhône Valley in France, California, or Australia, and it never ceases to evoke a positive response from me. Syrah is called Shiraz in Australia, but it's genetically identical. The wines are typically spicy and meaty and have a lively presence on the palate. These general characteristics form the bare minimum of what this grape can be. Drink this wine when you're feeling frisky. It typically has an intensity of fruit and more gamey and rustic qualities overall. Syrah is historically considered a manly man's wine, but, ladies, treat yourself to a glass. You won't be disappointed.

Merlot is a beautiful grape that was hit hard by Hollywood. The movie *Sideways* convinced everyone Merlot was a second-class grape. People began to see it as a Cabernet Sauvignon wannabe or generally producing crappy wine, when, in all reality, Merlot is a grape that produces richly colored, full-bodied, and flavorful wines that can feel velvety on the palate. Merlot is a grape famous for blue fruit (plums, figs, blueberries) driven and dense wines of Bordeaux, Napa Valley, Washington, and even Italy. Merlot is most certainly worth further exploration.

Something to keep in mind: For the grapes I briefly described, their styles and nuances will change depending on where the vines are grown in the world. Even more so, the way different producers decide to treat the individual grape varieties will impact the finished wines.

What makes red, white, rosé, sweet, and sparkling wine all different?
The way winemakers obtain different kinds of wines is mainly due to what grapes they use to make the wine, how the juice is fermented into wine, and various decisions the winemaker makes after fermentation (e.g., aging wine in a barrel before bottling).

A red wine, for example, obtains its color using the skin of red grapes. Grape juice is always clear, so a red wine had grape skin contact during fermentation, while a white wine didn't see any skin contact. Winemaking can be complicated and extensive, but there are understandable ways to break it all down.

Once again, red wine is the clear juice of red grapes that has been fermented with the grape skins. By fermenting the clear juice with the skin, the skin pigments, or colors, the juice and adds additional flavors and compounds.

White wine is the clear juice of white grapes that has been separated from the skins after the grapes were pressed (the method of squeezing juice out of grapes). The juice is fermented without skin contact. This is why the wine is different shades of "white" and isn't quite as hardy or structured as red wine.

Rosé describes a style of wine made using mainly red grapes and potentially some white as well. Essentially, you wouldn't be able to achieve the pink color without at least a bit of red grape skin.

Many people think rosé is a certain kind of grape, but it is simply a term to describe how the wine is made. Limiting the amount of time the juice spends in contact with the skin results in a blush or pink color. There are several ways to limit the contact between the skins and the juice. For now, just think, *Less skin contact with juice equals rosé instead of red wine*, and you will be ahead of the game.

Sweet wine is another category of wine, and *sweet* is a somewhat misused term. A lot of wine lovers think any wine with a big fruit character or mouth-filling body is "sweet." In reality, a sweet wine has to have a good amount of what's called *residual sugar*. This fancy word is just saying the juice is fermented in a way that intends for leftover sugar to be experienced on the palate. Producers can get a good raw product to make a sweet wine by letting the grapes ripen longer than they would let them ripen for a regular dry wine. By having much more sugar when they harvest the grapes, it allows them to ferment the juice enough to obtain the desired alcohol level. Then, while there is still a healthy amount of sugar left in the juice, they can stop the fermentation.

One main way a winemaker can stop fermentation is by cooling down the fermenting juice. When fermenting juice is cooled, the yeast dies and stops converting sugar into alcohol. By stopping the fermentation in this way, a sweet wine could still have a 9 to 15 percent alcohol level and around 60 g/l residual sugar, for instance. In contrast, dry wines typically have closer to 3 g/l of residual sugar left in the finished wine. You are certainly meant to feel the sugar on your palate when it comes to sweet wines and their level of leftover sugar.

Sparkling wine is produced using the juice of either white or red grapes. A sparkling wine's character is determined by how a winemaker chooses to ferment the juice, what grapes are used, and where the grapes are grown. The primary goal of creating bubbly is to find a way to trap the alcohol and carbon dioxide that results from fermentation.

A winemaker can ferment the juice inside a big metal tank with a closed top to trap the carbon dioxide and alcohol. They would then pump the finished bubbles into a bottle and seal the bottle with a cork and metal cage. The winemaker can even use the bottle itself to ferment the juice and trap all the carbon dioxide and alcohol inside. This is called the *traditional method*. It's the most interesting, time-consuming, and elegant way to make sparkling wine. On the opposite end of the spectrum, producers can synthetically shoot a wine up with carbon dioxide. This would be the not-so-impressive sparkling wine we drank in college.

What are legs?

I have found *legs* to be a trigger word among people in my wine classes. Many have attended a dinner party where the "wine expert" goes on and on about the legs of a wine. The self-proclaimed expert makes sure the whole table recognizes his wine superiority by pointing to the drops of liquid running down the sides of the glass. Everyone thinks the person must be a true source of wine knowledge because he speaks about the *legs*. Yet he typically never explains what the legs actually represent or speaks any further about the wine's quality.

Don't be the leg guy! My first encounter with this type of wine person was back when I was mixing Crystal Light into red wine. Clearly, I was susceptible to wine-expert imposters. I was at a wine bar with an older, affluent crowd back in my college days and trying to take in all the wine knowledge I could.

One particular gentleman took on the role of Condescending Wine Expert. I listened adamantly as he showed me the seemingly "magical" legs on the sides of my glass. After that night, I thought the only factor determining quality in wine were the legs. My legs allusion was soon busted as I gained more wine education.

I came to find out the drips of liquid on the sides of the glass, or legs, were simply a rough way to tell how much alcohol is in the wine. The fatter and slower moving the legs, the more alcohol in the wine. The thinner and faster moving the legs, the less alcohol in the wine. The basic premise behind this is that alcohol evaporates faster than water and the legs are the signs of leftover water after the alcohol evaporates out.

This being said, the amount of alcohol in a wine hardly tells you its true quality. There is so much more to wine than roughly judging how much alcohol it has from the legs. Legs are interesting to look at, but don't rely on them.

What makes wine good?

I am constantly asked this question. I have slowly started to figure out what good wine is to me. I consider good wine to be, above all things, balanced. That's a pretty vague word, *balanced*. When all the elements—the smells, flavors, and structure—come together in a pleasing way, it's a balanced wine. In other words, the wine isn't overly perfumed and lacking in character when you taste it. It isn't completely dominated by earthy, funky flavors when you drink it. It doesn't have a screaming-high alcohol content that takes away from any subtly in the wine.

I want to be intrigued by a wine and let it tell me a story of where it came from. I want to be able to taste that someone cared enough to make a wine in a quality-minded way. Ultimately, the only true measure of good wine is up to you. If you like a wine, then it's good and that's all that matters.

2

Twist of Fate

THE FUNNY THING WAS, DEEP DOWN I had visions of spending my life working with wine, but it couldn't have been further from my college major. My degree from UF wasn't in wine passion, but rather in advertising. As a young twenty-two-year-old woman, it seemed like an unattainable dream to pursue such an unconventional path. I kept imagining the raised eyebrows of everyone around me if I ever mentioned wanting to work with wine. Fear crept in and steered me away from thinking I could live that kind of life. I knew wine made me feel unlike anything else in the world. The feeling wasn't just about being tipsy either. It was deeper than that. Every smile from someone I exposed to wine made the passion grow inside me. However, spirit depleting as it was, I resolved I would have to move on to a "real world" job after graduation.

As I was applying for advertising jobs, I felt like a small part of me was dying. I knew that as soon as I got behind an office desk, I would start to lose the passion I had found. I predicted something in me would change. The light I wanted to bring to the world would slowly start to dim.

Sadly, I knew society expected me to get a job matching my major. I was supposed to build a normal career for the rest of my life. I required a kind of job that would give me a safe, secure, and comfortable life. I accepted it, despite my uneasiness. With three months before my graduation from college, everything looked all set on paper. I had promising job interviews lined up, and it looked as though my normal life would come to fruition. Regardless, I couldn't have been more afraid—not afraid of going out into the world, but of going out into the world to spend my life working toward something void of any real passion.

During the time of my hunt for a job and my presumed future, I experienced roommate issues, which were exactly what I didn't need. The tensions between my roommate and me began to intensify. The breaking point of our relationship came one early morning a month before graduation. The previous night, I had overheard my roommate on the phone saying horrible things about me to another friend. Part of me wanted to let it go, graduate, and move on. But another part wanted her to know she couldn't do that to people. I decided to confront her.

I waited for her to start banging around the kitchen before she left for her classes. I heard cabinets slam and made my move. I walked into the kitchen to let her know I'd heard what she had said about me. I caught her right as she was opening the front door to leave. I stopped her and let her know that if she was going to talk badly about me, she might want to make sure I wasn't awake in the room next to her.

I didn't know how she would react. It was the first time I really stood up for myself. I hated confrontation, but I felt empowered by the fact that I wouldn't stand by while she dragged my name through the dirt. Part of me thought she would just apologize and talk the situation over. What happened next was something I never saw coming.

Her eyes grew large and stormy. I stood my ground, prepared for any insult she could sling at me. Then she unloaded five minutes of verbal insults, the likes of which I had never experienced. She knew exactly what to say to tear at my heart. She said everyone talked badly about me, I wasn't a good friend, I had no future, and anything else she could think of to discredit what I was constantly striving to achieve in my life.

At first, I tried to defend myself, but eventually I just became a punching bag. As someone who valued friendships and only wanted to have a positive impact on the world, every hateful comment she spat at me felt like a blow to my stomach.

She brought my parents into it. She judged them for how they had raised me. I couldn't fathom where all this hatred was coming from. I was almost more confused than anything. I said nothing. The situation turned into me standing in a dark kitchen in my pajamas trying the hardest in my life not to cry.

The very last words she ever said to me were, "You're nobody."

I will never forget the pure meanness in her eyes, demanding me to fight back. I did nothing. She whipped around to leave. With the slam of the front door, I felt warm tears run down my cheeks. I wish I could say the exchange we shared had no effect on me at all. More so than the lingering emotional impact, the aftermath left me questioning my future. It forced me to reevaluate the entire direction of my life. It was as if I was crying less about her and more about the uncertainty I felt.

I called the one person who was always able to comfort me in my most difficult times. My mom picked up the phone in her usual upbeat way. I desperately wished I could hide the pain I was in. Unfortunately, I couldn't find the strength to hide anything at all. I told her everything that had just happened with my roommate between sobs.

I could tell by the tone of her voice that she felt my distress. She would've done anything to heal my sadness. She implored me to let her come down to be with me. I wouldn't agree to her dropping everything to drive two hours to comfort me. I let her know I'd be fine and not to worry. I could feel the emptiness in the words as I said them. We ended our conversation with her telling me how much she loved me. She promised everything was going to be all right. For the first time in my life, I wasn't so sure about that. I managed to break the shaking in my voice to tell her I loved her too. I was still so deeply hurt and wished I had let her come.

I should've known nothing would keep her from coming to the rescue. Two hours later, she called me from the parking lot of my apartment building. My mom will always be my hero for many reasons, and that afternoon was one of them. Her ability to bring humor to even the most hopeless situations shined during a day I didn't believe had the potential to be salvaged. She told me to come on down for a mother-daughter lunch.

Before we hung up, she said to bring the coffeemaker. It was a strange request, but it made me let out a much-needed laugh. My roommate loved coffee more than life itself. The communal coffeemaker for the apartment had been my contribution. A huge smile stretched across my face as I unplugged the machine. I made my way downstairs and stood in the parking garage with the coffeemaker in my arms.

My mom's car whipped around the corner and sped toward me like a shining beacon of light. She stopped, popped the trunk, and told me to toss the machine in. Next thing I knew, she wrapped her arms around me, and nothing could hurt me in that moment. Sitting at lunch, the dramatic situation inspired a deep conversation between us. I started to let her in on my fears for the future. I told her about the uneasiness

I had been hiding about my next steps in life. She asked me a simple question: "What would you do if you could do anything?"

Everyone fantasizes about their answer to this question. Of course I had dreamed up my answer. I stared away for a moment. I knew exactly what I wanted, but felt as though I shouldn't want it. I had never said my answer out loud. However, the day's events inspired me to be bold.

I told her I would go to Napa Valley, work at a winery, learn about wine, and be around people all day. I looked back and met her stare. I had anticipated her eyes would reflect some kind of empty disbelief. I expected her to tell me kindly that it wasn't possible. I thought she would encourage me to use my degree and get a "real job." There were a myriad of reasons she could have presented to me to give up on this fantasy. Instead, her eyes were hopeful and encouraging.

She said, "Do it." She told me she and my dad believed in me no matter what.

Something inside me changed at my mom's vow of confidence in my dream. In a matter of hours, I went from being a wounded soul to a believer. From the moment my mom supported my journey to discover wine, I never stopped believing anything was possible.

Wine Talk: Restaurants and Dinner Parties

For some, restaurants and social situations present the ideal opportunity to show off their wine prowess. In my early days working with wine, I wanted to show the world how much I knew. Showing off with wine never ends well. I was at a New York wine event at a high-end restaurant and was seated among other wine professionals. I figured I would take this opportunity to interject my knowledge about certain wines that were being poured. We were served a glass of champagne, and I attempted to engage the whole table with my thoughts on the wine. I went on and on about what I thought I knew. I talked about the flavor profile, the geography of where the grapes were grown, the producer's winemaking style, and anything else I could think of to give myself credibility.

After going on entirely too long I looked up from my glass hoping for nods of approval and engagement. I was met with unenthusiastic stares. One of my fellow dinner guests went so far as to subtly correct most of what I had said. I later found out I was seated, unknowingly, with several master sommeliers.

In general, sommeliers have a strong grasp on the knowledge of the various wine regions in the world. They can proficiently taste wine and determine its quality. Most importantly, they know how to expertly pair wine with food and gracefully serve it at a restaurant. That being said, a master sommelier is someone who has passed the highest level of certification a sommelier is capable of. Think of them as the Yodas of wine. These master sommeliers had more wine knowledge in their little pinkies than I had in my entire body.

I swallowed a huge dose of humility that night. At the end of the day, enjoying wine with others isn't a contest of who knows more or an opportunity to build one's self up. Drinking wine socially should be elegant and in the spirit of sharing. By following a few simple guidelines, you will effortlessly become the wine connoisseur among your friends and family, and not the snob.

How should I order off of a wine list at a restaurant and still look knowledgeable?

An easy way to avoid embarrassment is not to try to impress everyone or seem like you are a superstar in wine. Even as someone who is dedicating her life to the study of wine, I continuously ask questions. Not knowing about wine is totally fine, and a desire to learn is wonderful, but a snooty wine novice who exudes an air of superiority isn't. So, if you are at a restaurant with a sommelier, use his or her knowledge and expertise.

Also, ask good questions to get good results. Don't pigeonhole yourself into a boring wine corner by asking for one specific grape variety or for wine from just one particular region. Expand your horizons. That's what wine is for!

Ask the sommelier for something he or she is excited about, or something similar but unique to your reliable favorites, or just something that will sing with your meals. Your sommelier will love you for presenting them a chance to flex their wine muscles. It's in appreciating that wine can have a meaningful place at the table that makes you knowledgeable.

What do I do when a sommelier presents the wine to me at a restaurant?
My first time experiencing this process was quite unsuccessful. I pretended I knew what I was doing as the sommelier presented me the wine I'd ordered for the table. The sommelier poured me a sip, and I stared at my glass. I wondered what actions would make me look wine savvy. As my mind raced, I heard the sommelier clear his throat as if to encourage me to taste the sip.

I was paralyzed by uncertainty and could only look up at him. He asked if I wanted to taste it. Stage fright took over, and it was as if I'd forgotten how to drink wine. I simply looked at the glass and looked up at him and nodded it was okay. As he poured for the rest of the table, I continued to wonder what the hell I was actually supposed to do during the intimidating process.

Here's what I wish I had known.

After you order, the sommelier is going to present the wine to the table and have you make sure the bottle is sound. She is going to pour you a little sip and wait. This is your chance to show that you know what you're doing. All I want you to do is grab that glass with authority, give it a quick swirl, smell it, and take a sip.

If everything seems reasonable, and it's the wine you want to enjoy for the evening, give the cool nod of approval and simply say, *Yes, this will be fine.* You will have successfully navigated the murky waters of wine in a fine-dining establishment simply using confidence.

Here's another tip: Say you take that first sip and the wine is not at all what you expected. For instance, something smells or tastes off, you don't like it, it's not what you intended to order, or it's not going to give you an enjoyable evening. This is your chance to tell the sommelier it's not the bottle you were hoping for and kindly request another. If she says no, this isn't a restaurant that values hospitality, and don't go back. Mind you, if you send a bottle back eight times, even the most gregarious of restaurants will have trouble taking you seriously. You can achieve the power of wine confidence, but don't abuse it.

On the same subject, there are certain elements to look for to pinpoint a bottle that's off. There are two main faults in wine you should keep a nose out for: TCA and oxidation. TCA is 2,4,6-trichloroanisole. A wine's cork can become tainted with TCA in the winery. If so, the cork's infection can impact the wine, making it smell like moldy cardboard or wet newspaper. You won't become sick from drinking it, but the wine will be completely stripped of its character and seem lackluster. Oxidation can occur if a wine bottle is exposed to too much heat or oxygen. If you order a younger wine, any sign of this is a fault. Look for stewed-fruit aromas and an overly dry or tired sensation in the wine's flavors.

In a perfect restaurant world, there will be a sommelier to help guide you through the wine list, serve your wine, and pair it with your meals. However, that's not always the case. In this instance, your server will act as your pseudo sommelier. It's up to you to deeply inquire about the wine list, suggestions, and pairings. A high-quality server will most likely be able to guide you, but if not, you should respectfully request assistance from a manager or wine director, who will have more knowledge under their belt. It's not rude to do this; instead, it suggests to the staff that you have a higher interest in wine than the average dinner guest.

How can I be the ideal dinner-party guest or host with wine?

Impressing friends with wine at a dinner party is a subject of particular concern for a lot of people. Many of those who come to my classes and visit wine stores across the country want guidance in this department.

Do I buy something expensive just for the sake of it? Do I get something cheap and hope no one notices?

My best advice for this case is to buy a unique bottle of wine. Ask the wine shop steward for an exciting and crowd-pleasing grape that not many people have heard of. This will make the bottle both moderately priced and expand all your friends' palates. Unlike a Napa Cab that will cost an arm and a leg, a red wine from, say, Sardinia, Sicily, or Croatia will be interesting and delicious at half the price. This is because fewer people are familiar with these wines and the smaller demand helps keep the costs reasonable.

So, you are throwing a dinner party for six and have no idea how much wine is reasonable. The worst thing in the world is to be short on wine and leave your guests underwhelmed. The old standby I always use is to have at least one bottle on hand for each guest. If you are having ten people over, grab a variety of ten bottles. You may not drink it all, but this estimation will ensure everyone has a chance to feel a pleasant wine buzz.

In the sense of a dinner party, assume you will be slowly eating and drinking throughout the entire evening. By being prepared with the right amount of wine, the night will certainly go off without a hitch.

What are some good tips for pairing wine and food?

The easiest way to think about pairing food and wine is to go with the three *C*s. These tips can be your general guidelines for thinking about what you could drink with a meal.

The first *C* is to **complement**. When you try to complement food and wine, you are trying to match the flavors and structure of the wine to the flavors and structure of the food. An example of this would be pairing a Sauvignon Blanc with shrimp salad finished with citrus dressing. Sauvignon Blanc's citrus-filled flavors and mouth-watering nature are what makes this pairing magical. This wine will make the shrimp pop with flavor in the salad and still keep your palate refreshed after each sip due to the acid. Acid is the component of wine causing your mouth to water. In this way, each sip cleanses your palate and gets you ready for the next bite.

The next *C* is to **contrast**. When trying to make a successfully contrasting pairing, pick foods and wines at somewhat opposite ends of the spectrum. It's as though you are taking things that don't line up flavor- or structure-wise but can create balance in each other. An example of this would be pairing an off-dry Riesling and spicy food. The extra sugar in the wine cools down the meal, while the salty flavors in the dish bring out the fruit flavors in the wine and take the focus off the sugar in the wine.

The last *C* is to **compensate**. Say you have a red wine that is too aggressive and just doesn't taste pleasing to you. You may be able to fix this. You can pair this red wine with a rich cheese or fatty meat, and the wine will soften out. It will become a bit more flavorful due to the proteins breaking down the tannins (bitter, drying sensations) in the wine on your palate.

This can work both ways. Say you're having a dish that lacks acid or a certain brightness. You can actually use wine to enliven a meal. For instance, you can pair something like an Albarino to a bland fish dish and watch it transform due to the wine's bright acid and flavor profile.

A simple understanding of these basic premises can give you inspiration to play around with wine and food pairing. The best way to get better at pairing wine and food is to take on the mentality of an Italian: only drink wine when you eat and only eat when you drink wine.

3

"Impossible" Dream

BELIEVING I COULD DO SOMETHING and actually manifesting it were two very different things. I learned this lesson after I made up my mind to pursue my Napa Valley dream. My mind was on fire with the thoughts of moving in that direction for my life, but I knew the path was right. With conviction, I chased after it persistently; I was a woman on a mission. It didn't make what I wanted to achieve easy, but rather I was driven by a purpose. Having a purpose is a lot more effective than having an obligation. The first step was to be able to say, *Napa is my future*, but the real trick was making it a reality.

An advertising major from the University of Florida isn't exactly on every winery's hiring radar. What I really needed was someone to give me a shot. I was naïve in thinking any winery halfway across the country would share my same sense of risk-taking. I thought there must be tons of wineries willing to give this Florida girl a chance. I wrote up a letter describing my aspirations to implore Napa wineries to hire me.

I laid my heart on the line and packed the letter full of passion and soul. I sent it out to fifty wineries I had looked up online. Then, I waited for the job offers to start flying in. Five wineries actually wrote me back. Just five. Of the five, three told me it just wasn't going to be the right fit. I could've taken this as a sign of failure, and that the wine path wasn't meant to be. I clung to the other two wineries who wrote me back with every ounce of strength I had. One of the wineries was Orin Swift and the other was Inglenook. A dark thought in the back of my head whispered they wouldn't want me.

Three weeks before graduation, I had no job offers, no substantial plan, and just two wineries willing to even entertain the idea of me working for them. My parents never let me lose faith in myself. My dad wasn't willing to let me feel like I had no hope. He offered the backup plan of just coming home for the summer and then working out a job in wine country. The feeling of always knowing you can go home is reassuring and comforting, but the thought of walking across the stage for graduation jobless, homeward bound, and without my Napa adventure added greater resilience to my pursuit.

Orin Swift had set up a phone interview with me, and Inglenook wanted to interview me via Skype. My first interview was with Orin Swift, and everything went well enough. I was honest in my lack of any formal wine knowledge or experience. They were kind enough to humor a young girl with lofty aspirations. At the end of my babbling on about a yearning to learn and what I could bring to Orin Swift, they let me down easy. They politely said it would be best if I sat down with them in person once I moved to the valley. They wanted me to get settled into Napa and then see if there might be an entry-level position for me. Even I couldn't justify heading off into the horizon without a real job. I had to know something was waiting for me if I made my move to California. It appeared Inglenook was the only shimmer of light keeping my dream alive.

I can still hear the ring of the Skype call from Inglenook HR a few days after my Orin Swift interview. My heart was pounding, as this felt like my last chance. I accepted the call, and two women appeared on my computer screen. With a slightly bad connection, we started the interview. Helen and Jenna introduced themselves, and in my mind, they held the keys to my future. I went into my usual self-sell, but something felt different this time. I was more authentic and honest, and my answers to their questions weren't forced or overdone. At the end of the interview, we had talked for fifteen minutes. They let me know they were looking at a few other candidates and that they would get back to me. Helen said they would know in about two weeks who would get the job. We said our goodbyes and my screen went black. Questions rushed into my mind. Did they like me? Who are these other candidates? Will Inglenook be my future? The interview gave me two things: unanswered questions and hope.

A week and a half went by, and I had resolved to enjoy the last few weeks of college and my friends. It's really all I could do. My grand finale of the UF night scene was a bar-hopping event called Gator Stompin'. I absolutely did some stompin'. That night was a time for me to see all the people I shared so many memories with. It was a chance to say farewell to all the bars and restaurants that had filled my college experience with its fair share of enjoyment. I took a "party smart" pill, which was supposed to prevent a hangover. I thought I could drink whatever I wanted because of the magic pill. With that, I was all set to give UF its proper goodbye.

The only problem with the nostalgic and festive night was that I hadn't eaten and there were a lot of spots to relive with a lot of alcohol to consume. The gravity of all the change, uncertainty, and waiting to hear back from Inglenook made me tip each glass back a bit more freely. The last thing I remember is jumping up and down to "Shout" at one of my favorite bars. Next thing I remember is being "that girl" with arms flung around my friends, being helped into a car and taken home.

I woke up the next day at 2:00 p.m. with Gatorade and a waste basket by my side. I had several firsts that morning. It was the first time I had ever slept that late, the first time I was sloppy drunk, and the first time I felt like I might not be able to move for days from such a hangover. As my head continued to spin, my mom texted me that she and my dad had just arrived in Gainesville. My parents were there for my graduation happening the next morning. Their timing was simply impeccable.

I summoned every ounce of strength and took the longest shower of my life. I threw on a dress and made my way to my parents' hotel to convince myself and them that everything was fine. When I saw them, I stayed as upbeat as possible and didn't happen to mention that I still had what felt like gallons of alcohol coursing through my veins. My gigi arrived later that afternoon. Of course I love my grandma, but at times Gigi and I didn't see eye to eye on things. I had a feeling my lack of employment after graduation wouldn't sit well with her. Along with the copious thoughts swirling in my head, I had nearly given up on Inglenook.

Despite my personal emotional roller coaster, we all ventured out to my favorite Italian restaurant in Gainesville to celebrate my graduation. I drove everyone there, dropped them at the front of the restaurant, and pulled away to find parking. After grabbing a spot on the street and yanking the key out of the ignition, I just sat there and took a deep breath. I didn't feel deserving of any kind of celebrating, not to mention I wasn't quite ready for what it looked like my life was shaping up to be. As I resolved to get on with the show, my phone began to ring. I saw a 707 area code, which I thought must have been a wrong number. I stared at my phone for a moment, but then reached for my door handle. Right before I stepped out of the car, the dots connected in my brain that 707 was the area code for a California number.

I lunged for my phone and picked it up with an almost out-of-breath greeting. The voice of Helen from Inglenook greeted me, and I stopped breathing all together. We exchanged pleasantries, and I desperately wished she would give me a chance to change the course of my life forever. She was offering me the position of a bistro associate. I knew that pretty much meant I would be starting at the bottom of the barrel in the wine world, but none of that mattered. This was the small foot in the door I had been praying for. She went into compensation and all the formalities, but all that kept echoing in my head were the words "We'd like to offer you the position."

Her important question snapped me back into reality: "Would you like to accept the position?"

Looking back, I did everything wrong. I didn't ask for a day to think, I didn't negotiate salary, and I don't think I even let her finish the question. It was as if none of those details mattered because I had never been surer of anything in my life. I said yes, and she wished me a happy graduation. For the first time in months, I felt certain it would be.

The feelings of grogginess, slowness, and lukewarm excitement for the future were transformed into elation. A spark of life shot through me and has stayed with me ever since. I quite literally ran into the restaurant to tell my parents. I turned a corner to find them calmly perusing the menu. Having the chance to tell them in person was a gift, which I didn't intend to waste. I looked them both in the eyes and told them I got the job in Napa. I assured them Inglenook was my future. I waited for them to process what I had shared, and I braced for their reactions. Their expressions would color my entire outlook on my next chapter. What their faces said would tell me if I had made a wise decision or the worst mistake of my life. Their eyes lit up, and they were genuinely proud of me. I wish I could relive that moment over and over. My parents and I shared joint excitement and reveled in the moments of celebration.

Gigi had the exact opposite reaction. Her look was more a mix of confusion and disapproval. She started in on the questions.

"Why would you go work in wine?"

"How much are you making?"

"You two aren't really going to let her do this?"

"Where will you live?"

"Who do you know in Napa?"

"What kind of career will you have in wine?"

All these questions were meant to convince me I had chosen the wrong path. My grandma represented every normal person in the world who wouldn't see sense in taking this path. She was every person who lacked vision and whose aspirations were to get a steady job close to home. My parents and I knew it wasn't me to take the safe and well-worn path. With each question, my smile grew wider. With each narrow-minded, disbelieving comment, I knew I was venturing further from a bland, humdrum outlook on life. My parents gave me the spirit to go after something more out of life, and Inglenook gave me the chance to create the life I had been yearning for. My responsibility was then and always will be not to waste a single moment in pursuing what I love.

Wine Talk: How to Taste Wine

When it comes to learning to taste wine, everyone has to start from the bottom. There can be many moments of frustration and feelings of impossibility when describing a glass of wine. My first few months in a tasting group were rampant with feelings of failure. Week after week

I attended tastings, and I felt like the wine would just never speak to me. I searched the glass using my nose and palate and never found anything. Unbeknownst to me, my nose and palate were getting stronger after each "failure."

One of my first moments when everything started to click involved the aroma and flavor of green pepper. Indeed, green pepper saved me from giving up on tasting wine completely. I had a deep-purple wine in my glass that fateful day. I stuck my nose in the glass half expecting the same empty thoughts that had filled my mind every previous week. Then, I smelled green pepper as if someone had sliced it and put it right up to my nose. I almost dropped the glass in amazement. I tasted it, and the same dominant flavor danced across my palate. I later learned the aromas and flavor of green pepper can be associated with a Cabernet Sauvignon, and that had been the wine in my glass.

I realized wine had always been revealing itself to me; I just needed to keep practicing to know how to understand it. Learning to fully appreciate and taste wine is a long and slow process. The beauty is that it's an attainable skill. It all starts with an open mind and a willingness to be wrong—a lot. It will all be worth it when wine starts speaking to you and you're able to translate what it's saying.

Why do people care so much about the pretentious wine-tasting process?

To the untrained eye, wine tasting seems to be quite pretentious. Non-wine people don't understand what wine tasters are doing when they seemingly obsess over a glass of wine.

However, the main goal of purposefully tasting a wine is to learn about its character in a somewhat objective and measurable way. We look at, smell, and taste a wine to gather information about what we are drinking. Collecting clues and learning about wine make it ten times more enjoyable. By doing this over and over with wines from all over the world, you can learn to detect differences in quality and style.

For instance, if you repeatedly taste glasses of good-quality Riesling you'll start to develop an understanding of the wine's character. You'll know the wine should be crystal clear and almost white in color. It will smell of stone fruits, honeysuckle, a slight smokiness, and fresh stream water, and will taste balanced with a touch of sugar alongside a mouth-watering acid. Your mind's eye will start envisioning Riesling's character in this way. So, if you are poured a glass of Riesling directly opposite of all these characteristics, you will know it's not the best quality wine. Vice versa, if you are poured a glass that elegantly portrays the characteristics of a quality example, you know you are in for a well-made glass of wine.

What do you search for when you smell?

A lot of people are very intimidated by smelling or think their noses are broken. This is just not true. Whatever you smell in a glass of wine is your opinion, and you shouldn't be ashamed of that. One way to get better at smelling is to work out your nose. Smell all the time. Smell everything you possibly can. This is one way to make your nose more sensitive to the aromas in wine without anything too technical or complicated.

Smelling a glass of wine for more than a few seconds may seem unnatural, but by taking the time to really dive into a glass, you can discover aromas you had been missing. The best way to smell a glass of wine is to fully immerse your nose into the opening of the glass. Take a few strong whiffs and take your nose out again. Think about what smells filled your mind, and then put your nose in the glass once again and try to find the same smells or new ones. Doing this with every glass of wine will naturally help you strengthen your wine-smelling abilities.

When discussing the smells of wine, it's vital to understand what they really are and where they come from. What if I told you the only real fruits in your glass were grapes? People get confused because when wine professionals write and talk about wine, they laundry list things like fruits, spices, flowers, and rocks. To an onlooker, this must mean winemakers infuse these real elements in the wine somehow. This isn't true.

The aromas you are smelling in wine are mainly the result of volatilized compounds due to fermentation that each grape genetically carries. The grape genetics, in general, provide the main aroma profile for what's in your glass. We give volatilized compounds more understandable and conversational names instead of their scientific terms. This is where people get confused.

Additionally, when you add in climate, vineyard, and winemaker decisions, you can have different expressions of the same grape variety. For instance, Pinot Noir from France doesn't smell exactly the same as one from California. A myriad of factors change the potential character of every wine, and that's something to always keep in the back of your mind.

The main categories of smells you should look for in a glass of wine are fruits, non-fruits (flowers, herbs, spices, oak), and minerality (smells of rocks, dirt, earth). By focusing on the individual categories, you can help focus your mind and nose on what to look for in wine.

How do you go about sipping wine the correct way?
There is a fair amount of noise and hoopla that goes into tasting wine, but everything is for a reason. The best way to get the most out of tasting a wine on your palate is to start with taking a nice big sip. There are several things to look for when having a wine on your palate. See if the wine flavors match what you smelled on the nose. Look for the feel, or texture, of the wine. Also, search for the wine's structure (i.e., acid, tannin, and body; these elements will be defined in greater detail in the next section).

To do these things, hold the wine on your palate before swallowing. Then things get tricky. I want you to try to almost roll the wine on your tongue while taking in air. This part may require some practice. The reason for this seemingly awkward step is to make sure as much air as possible is hitting the wine even when it's in your mouth. By doing this, the wine's flavors and aromas will be released more fully onto your palate. Basically, your wine will be more alive.

After that comes the mouthwash technique. You want to literally swish the wine around to hit every single part of your mouth. You will get a greater appreciation for the overall structure and feel of a wine. Then drink that baby down. By drinking wine in this seemingly complex way, you will set yourself up to experience the fullest range of flavors, textures, and structural elements in the wine.

What am I actually looking for on my palate when I taste a glass of wine?

Tasting wine can seem vastly complicated for someone just wanting a basic understanding of wine. That's why I like to focus on just a few main things when tasting wine, instead of throwing around excessive babble.

First thing I look for is if the wine is dry, off-dry, or sweet. I use the tip of my tongue to tell if there is leftover sugar in the wine. A little bit of sugar would be considered off-dry, and if you feel a lot of sugar, the wine could potentially be sweet. To lock in what leftover sugar feels like, buy a bone-dry Riesling and a sweet Riesling (your local wine shop can help you pick). Taste them side by side, and you can lock in what sugar does and doesn't feel like when you taste it in wine.

After I feel for sweetness, I think about the overall character of the wine. Is it laser sharp and going straight down the middle of my palate? That would be a lean style. Does it have a riper feeling and envelop my whole mouth? That would be a rounded style. Questions like these help me figure out a wine's overall texture.

Then things get a bit more technical. We can start thinking about the actual physical effects of wine on our palate. The three key elements I want you to know are acid, tannin, and body.

Acid is in every grape and thus is present in different amounts in every finished wine. "Acid" may sound off-putting, but it's the electric sharpness running through wines. Feel for it by noticing how much you are salivating or if you feel a prickle on your tongue. Wines will have more or less acid depending on climate (cooler equals more acid) and the grapes' genetics (some grapes are predisposed to higher levels upon harvest).

Everyone's heard of tannins, yet many people just have no clue what they are. **Tannins** are compounds that come mostly from the skin of the grapes. They can only be *felt*. Saying you can look at wine and tell it will be tannic or smell the tannins is a surefire way to indicate you are a wine novice. Tannins give you the sensation of something drying your mouth out. They will be felt mostly on your gums, tongue, and the sides of your mouth. A wine has more or less depending on a grape's skin or if the wine was aged in a barrel. Those are two main sources of tannins in wine.

Finally, I feel for the wine's body. **Body** is the weight of the wine on your palate. For instance, if you can compare the weight of wine to the feel of skim milk, it's light bodied. If you can compare the weight of the wine to 2 percent milk, it's medium bodied. Finally, if the wine feels the same weight of cream, it's full bodied.

Why do wine people spit?
The first thing people wonder about with formal tastings is what's going on with all the spitting. They believe people are insane for spitting out perfectly good wine. The reason wine professionals do it is because they don't want to get drunk.

Easy enough right? Say a wine professional has over eighty wines to try for a tasting. Swallowing all that wine would lead to a stomach pump, no doubt. So we learn everything we can from a wine and then simply spit it out. Being sober really helps when you are trying to study and learn from the wines in front of you. I learned this lesson especially quickly after my first tasting in Napa.

I was presented with several wines and a little white cup to spit into. I thought they were clearly just messing with me. As I focused on learning as much as I could from the wines, I took sip after sip. The sound of wine splashing into cups broke my concentration. I looked around and realized most of my wine was gone and everyone was spitting away. Needless to say, my wine buzz didn't help with my wine analysis and made me way too much fun for a wine tasting. After this realization, the foreign exercise of spitting out the wine wasn't exactly a raging success either. My best advice—practice spitting. Your wine tasting will improve immensely.

4

Two Women and Thousands of Miles

I HEARD MY DAD SLAM THE TRUNK SHUT on my life's possessions. It was amazing how my entire life fit into a two-door car. I glanced over at my mom in the driver's seat. She had resolved to take her daughter across the country with an unwavering smile on her face. It must've been unsettling to know she would be dropping me off in a completely foreign place to fend for myself. Despite her inevitable unease, fear, and anxiety on behalf, my mom decided she would be by my side for the cross-country trek to Napa Valley. My dad, no doubt, shared my mom's apprehension for the unknown. However, he, too, pushed doubts aside to make sure I knew he believed in me.

The last thing my dad said to me was, "Go make something happen."

I promised him I would.

Our Napa trek was our first cross-country journey, but certainly not our first road trip.

When I was in college, we went on one particularly unforgettable journey. We drove up to Williamsburg and Washington, D.C., from Jacksonville. It was the first trip my mom and I took together just the two of us. My mom traditionally traveled cautiously. She wasn't exactly the biggest risk-taker for the majority of my life up until that point. She preferred to go places she was familiar with and always made sure my dad stayed by her side. I had begged her to take the trip with me up the East Coast. Although apprehensive, she agreed.

It's not like we were going skydiving or anything, but for the first time, I saw my mom as fearless. She embraced the trip and focused more on the possibilities for enjoyment instead of what might go wrong.

We took off at dawn one summer morning for our week up the East Coast. I put together a CD for us to listen to on the drive. I chose songs we both loved or ones that held a personal significance. One song in particular made us pause midconversation. The soulful melody overtook both of us. When the song ended, my mom needed to know where she had heard the music before. I reminded her the song was from a YouTube video I had shown her months previously.

The YouTube video was called "Where the Hell Is Matt?" and we had both been in tears together as we watched it. The video followed a man in various countries around the world doing a goofy dance. At first, he was alone, and the focus was more on the beautiful sights and the question of why this random man was dancing all around the world. In the second part the man revisited all the different countries, with the people who lived there rushing into the frame to dance with him. Our eyes started watering up as we took in the larger message of the video.

We realized we all had the ability to impact people. His small act of dancing brought people together, even if just for five minutes. We watched the young, old, black, Asian, white, disabled, and a myriad of others as they shared joy just by dancing. There was no concern for politics, money, or pride.

The video helped ingrain something into our minds. There was more hope of uniting people than dividing them. Even more importantly, one could create meaningful connections in even the simplest of ways. After rehearing the song in the car, we both had an unspoken need to make the trip more than just a trip. I told her it was going to sound crazy, but we could do something like the video. I wanted to do something that would make us forever remember our time together. I suggested we make a video exactly like "Where the Hell Is Matt." She excitedly agreed, and I realized the journey had suddenly become more than just a relaxing trip.

We worked out our plan during the hours on the road. At random parts of the trip we resolved to engage people and ask if they liked to dance. We would see if they agreed to be involved with a mother-daughter project we were doing. If they did, we would play music on a phone and have a bystander video it all. Then, we had it. We created our own small way to see if we could stir up people's lives for the better.

Our first stop was Williamsburg, Virginia, a historical reenactment park of sorts. We had gone there as a family in years gone by, and it held fond memories for us. We checked into a historical bed-and-breakfast, and the filming began. We must have spent an hour and a half rehearsing our dancing intro for the video we aspired to create. Everything hurt from laughing and performing cut after cut until our dance was "perfect."

The following day presented the task of actually finding people to take five minutes and dance with two complete strangers. My mom and

I were about to ask people to completely put down their inhibitions and share a dance with us in Williamsburg, Virginia.

We played Tourist for a while, taking in the sights of the sites. More importantly, we searched for our first dance partner. While on the hunt, we walked into a colonial shop and there was a woman dressed in traditional garb, dusting. She was a short, plump woman, and her facial expression can only be described as blah. She looked bored and disenchanted. I declared to Mom she was our first dancing recruit.

My mom tried to convince me this woman would no more dance with us than the man on the moon. I kept with my gut and approached the woman. She looked up at me and seemed poised to point me to this trinket or that. I pulled a fast one on her and asked her if she liked to dance. Moreover, I asked if she would help us out with a project. She stared blankly at me for a second, and I assumed she thought I was certifiably crazy. I turned, ready to grab my mom and book it out of there. Then, in an unexpected change of character, she answered that she loved dancing.

Never in my life have I seen someone come alive before my very eyes like our new colonial friend. We hit play on my cell phone, and the classic song "Shout" blared through the speakers. The three of us danced and laughed with no regard for the onlookers. Every second we danced, the woman shook off another cobweb that had accumulated in her soul.

We must have met and danced with fifteen people on that trip. We danced with a girl celebrating her sweet sixteen, the hotel bellman, a barista at a coffee shop, a worker at a kayak shop near the Potomac, and countless others. After we returned home, I put all the dancing clips together for our own YouTube video.

Whenever I watch the video we made, I remember what life is all about. Even if you can do nothing else, you have a chance to bring someone unexpected joy. We did it over and over on our road trip. My mom and I realized we could affect people, and they could affect us.

I snapped back to reality with the sight of the Welcome to Mississippi sign. The miles kept sliding by. We blazed through Mississippi, Texas, New Mexico, and Arizona. Then my mind drifted to my most recent memories. In the months between graduating and making my cross-country excursion, I backpacked through Europe with a best friend of mine.

Elle had always been the "yes" girl in college. She had jumped out of a plane with me, took spontaneous road trips, and had a similar contagious enthusiasm for life. We decided we had to trek through Europe together the summer after we graduated from UF.

I figured the current car ride provided as good a time as ever to tell my mom the stories of our European travels. Elle and I had traveled to twelve cities and seven countries, with just the backpacks on our backs for twenty-six days. We did all the stereotypical must-dos during our trip to Europe. We jumped from hostel to hostel, city to city, and I had never felt more alive. We saw the likes of London, Paris, Rome, Switzerland, Munich, and Prague. What I loved most about the whirlwind trip were the things I could've never imagined happening.

I filled the hours of driving alongside my mom with a highlight reel of the events that would forever be imprinted on my mind. I began telling my tales of our first stop in London. The iconic city was our introduction to Europe. We hit the ground running, going straight from Heathrow Airport to the streets of London.

The tube let us off at Westminster Abbey. There was no way I was even attempting to hide the fact that my mouth was visibly open for several minutes taking it all in. My first real taste of Europe was everything I had hoped for. Then, in our mesmerized state, we were practically pushed down by a police officer barricading the street in front of Westminster Abbey.

The police started getting everyone behind barricades, and we found ourselves on the side of the street in front of a growing crowd. We had no idea what was going on, but something worth sticking around for seemed to be happening. We asked a gentleman next to us what was going on, and he enthusiastically exclaimed the queen was coming.

Less than twenty-four hours in London and the queen was expected to pass right in front of our eyes. There were people who had lived in London their whole lives who had never seen her. We waited about fifteen minutes, and the royal caravan rolled slowly by us. I can still remember the diamonds sparkling in her crown. The queen's delicate wave welcomed us to what would turn out to be the trip of our lives.

Our journey wasn't exactly all posh. I figured my mom should hear some of the less glamorous stories from the unpredictable trip. During our stay in Italy, I made a minor miscalculation with train times, which led us to sleeping in the train station where no one spoke English. A homeless Italian gentleman shared the train station with us the whole night. To this day, I still don't remember what tiny train station in the middle of nowhere we were stranded in. Because of this, I can damn well sleep just about anywhere with ease.

Despite any set back, we just kept moving forward no matter what. Much like when I was with my mom, Elle and I used humor to survive Europe, even with intimidating train station dwellers.

Another particularly eventful stop for us was Nice, France. During our stay in the enchanting place, I started experiencing some serious lady problems. UTIs are never fun and especially not in a foreign country. At the time of the trip, I had no idea what was actually wrong with me as I had never had one before. All the symptoms convinced me I was somehow dying. I went to an ER in Nice and prepared for them to turn me away due to a lack of "emergency." To my surprise, they ushered me to the back and did a few tests to conclude it was, in fact, a UTI. I was relieved I wasn't dying, and the doctor seemed baffled seeing an enormous smile spread across my face after the diagnosis.

The French doctor wrote me a prescription and directed me to get it filled. The language barrier was so daunting I couldn't ask any questions about the medication or what it was. I took a UTI leap of faith and went to the pharmacy.

As I walked toward the neon-green cross indicating a pharmacy, I expected to pay hundreds of dollars for some unknown French medication. I handed a woman at the front desk the prescription and she fetched a container of powder. She mixed it with a cup of water and instructed me to drink it. The laissez-faire vibe of the experience caught me off guard, but not enough for me to avoid drinking it down the hatch.

I started fumbling for my wallet to pay whatever bill I had incurred. However, she waved my wallet away and sent me on my way. More astonishing than partaking in France's healthcare system was the power of the drug. After two hours, my body was completely healed. Because of the rapid recovery, Elle and I headed off to the Cannes Film Festival. I have no idea what I took, but if I ever get a UTI again, I hope it's in France.

As the tail end of our trip arrived, one of our last stops was Amsterdam. With our arrival to the final leg of the trip, we had experienced obstacles, challenges, and more jaw-dropping scenery than I ever knew possible. We navigated our way to our final hostel. More than anything, we needed to get our backpacks off and rest.

We had just been on an overnight train from Prague. I booked it because I had illusions of grandeur of a train ride across Europe. I had obviously misread the small print when I made our reservations, because it turned out Elle and I were seated in a train car made for two but carrying six people total.

Our four companions were all middle-aged, burly Germans who spoke no English. The comfy beds I was envisioning turned out to be fold-out cots all stacked on top of each other. Elle and I were assigned the bottom cots, and as we settled in to try to sleep, I glanced over at Elle. One of the Germans began taking off his pants about two inches from her face. At that moment, I believe she could have killed me. After an astounding three or so hours of sleep, we pulled into Amsterdam.

Our excitement was rekindled, and we shook off the hardships of the train ride from hell.

An American studying in Amsterdam greeted us at the hostel. She was very pleasant, and I gave her my name to check in. She stared back at me with a mix of horror and sadness. I assumed her reaction was due to the fact that we looked like weary travelers. Instead, she told me we weren't in the system. I knew there must have been some kind of mistake. I reviewed my booking documents, and sure enough, I had made the reservation for the wrong day. She was mortified for us and proceeded to call at least ten other hostels in the area for a room, but to no avail.

She kept apologizing as it was becoming clear that we might not have a place to sleep that night. She saw two young girls, in a foreign city, with nowhere to go, and she felt horrible for us. Elle and I looked at each other as if to say, *To hell with it.* We weren't about to let this bring us down. We had been through too much, seen too much, and grown too much in Europe. We smiled and thanked her profusely for her help. We told her Amsterdam was waiting, and it was a perfect day to see it.

She quite literally asked us who we were and how we weren't completely freaking out. We told her taking a situation in stride proved most effective for us. There were too many miraculous things to see in the world to focus on the horrible. Her mouth was still slightly ajar as we walked out to greet Amsterdam.

We ended up sleeping in the airport that night before our a.m. flight. I wouldn't have changed a thing during our time in Amsterdam. We had a chance to see what we were made of with one final challenge. I realized we were made of a lot.

Every new country, we grew a bit stronger. Every misstep, we grew thicker skin. Every breathtaking sight, we loved life more. The moment the plane landed back in the States was profound for me. As soon as the wheels hit the tarmac, I knew I wasn't the same person who left twenty-six days before. I had never experienced such a feeling of fulfillment. I felt I could've gone at any moment after that and died happy. It may be morbid, but it's still a miraculous thought that life could offer that kind of satisfaction. I watched my mom's fascination grow with each story. Granted, the borderline-homeless sleeping arrangements and health scares received "oh, dear God" facial expressions from her.

Another realization dawned on me as I discussed my European adventure. For the first time, I told curious strangers what I intended to do with my life. I'm not sure if it was mostly because of the enthusiasm I radiated as I told people, but people's eyes seemed to light up as I shared with them my future of working with wine in Napa Valley. In a way, I saw wine as my way to keep exploring and connecting with people.

As my mind kept wandering during the road trip, I implored myself never to lose the sense of adventure I had discovered. I knew I had to keep that spirit a part of me. Napa would be my way.

Wine Talk: The Art of Winemaking

My first monthly meeting at Inglenook, I was told Francis Ford Coppola was going to be in attendance. I assumed nothing else anyone said at the meeting would even distract me from being in the same room as the famous director. I was wrong.

During the first part of the meeting, my eyes were transfixed on the directing legend sitting in the corner. Then Philippe Bascaules, Inglenook's winemaker, started to speak. I was even more transfixed by his descriptions of how he'd gone about crafting the new vintage of Cabernet Sauvignon. He went into the decisions they'd made in the vineyards, how to decide when to harvest, the vinification techniques he used, the barrel aging, and his personal description of the resulting wine. His French pronunciation of the deep purple color, the layered aromas of blackberry, cigar, leather, licorice, coffee, and dried sage, and the plush but refined mouthfeel completely stole my attention away from Francis Ford Coppola.

I figured out during the meeting that winemaking was equal parts agriculture, science, and art. By understanding the art of winemaking, wine has the potential to capture even more of your imagination.

Other than winemaking and grape variety, can a winemaker make a wine taste different?

Even just scratching the surface, it is clear to see a winemaker has a distinct impact on the finished wine. So, to answer the question, yes. However, in my opinion, winemaking can't hide low-quality grapes. A winemaker is not a magician but more of a steward of the grapes a vineyard produces.

Let's take Pinot Noir for example. We have a wine made from grapes growing in Burgundy in the La Tâche vineyard owned by Domaine de la Romanée-Conti. No expense is spared in growing the highest-quality grapes possible. The winemaker watches the yields, proper irrigation, soil health, and any other imaginable detail. This, in unison with a year of great weather, provides some of the finest Pinot Noir grapes in the world. The resulting wine will have the potential for greatness because of these reasons. A winemaker will make sure to craft the grapes into a wine reflecting these attributes. The vineyard is what allows the winemaker to make a high-quality wine.

On the other end of the spectrum, you have a Pinot Noir vineyard in California that is heavily planted, overly irrigated, and on subpar land. The resulting grapes are overripe and lackluster and don't have any noticeable character. A winemaker can manipulate and try to make a finished wine taste better, but the wine will never be at the same level of the previously mentioned Burgundian wine. Thus, a winemaker is important, but where and how the grapes are grown are vital to the final quality of a wine.

What is fermentation?

The natural act of fermentation is what led ancient civilizations to believe wine was of the gods. Contrary to beer, in its earliest origins, grape juice appeared to bubble without the help of man and created an intoxicating beverage. What was happening then and what happens now is naturally occurring yeast converts the sugar from grape juice into alcohol while releasing heat and carbon dioxide.

The reason this process could happen naturally in the past was because wild yeasts live on the outside of grape skins. Of course, today, there are numerous other ways man can intervene with the process to create certain styles of wine. The beauty of wine, to me, is how a seemingly simple process can produce vastly fascinating wines.

Are red and white wines fermented differently?

The biggest considerations between red wine and white wine fermentation are the respective prefermentation musts, or the juice, and the temperature during fermentation. The decisions made about how to ferment the juice of grapes can have a huge impact on what kind of wine is created.

For white wine, in most cases (orange, or skin-contact white wine, is the exception), the skins are separated from the juice. Thus, all that is fermented is the clear white grape juice. This is why white wine only has subtle color in the glass.

For reds, in most cases, the skin is left in touch with the juice. The skins contribute the color, tannin, and structure for red wines. Also, this is why red wines take on more ruby and purple colors.

Temperature is the next consideration when fermenting juice into finished wine. White wine juice is fermented at lower temperatures to retain the fresher and more delicate style of whites. Reds are fermented at higher temperatures to extract more personality from the skins. Reds are hardier on the whole and can handle the increased temperatures. The more intense flavors and aromas originate from these higher temperatures.

Why do producers age their wines in a barrel?

Many people wonder what exactly barrel aging does to wine. Barrel aging can contribute many things to a finished wine, but I want to focus on the two main effects of using barrels. One benefit is to introduce small amounts of oxygen to a wine. The other is to have the flavors from the barrel incorporate into the wine. Both of these attributes affect white and red wine, but in slightly different ways.

White wines gain a slight depth and more yellow color from exposure to oak and oxygen. Winemakers choose specific grape varieties like Chardonnay and sometimes Sauvignon Blanc because their grape profiles can stand up to and benefit from the exposure, while wines like Riesling, Assyrtiko, and Torrontés classical won't see oak because they typically show better with a fresh and pure character.

Most red wines benefit from some oak and oxygen exposure. In general, red wines have more structure and tannin. *Structure* is a catchall term for a wine's weight, or body, and its presence on the palate. For reds, oxygen helps integrate, smooth out, and add flavors to a wine. Cabernet Sauvignon, Merlot, and Malbec typically see oak usage because of their higher structure and tannin.

In regard to flavor contribution from a barrel, Chardonnay and Sauvignon Blanc grapes gain nuttiness, buttered-popcorn aromas, spiciness, and added creamy texture. Cabernet Sauvignon, Merlot, and Malbec grapes gain vanilla, smoke, baking spice, and a plush mouthfeel. The different effect of oak on white versus red wine all comes down to the structure of each respective wine. Due to Chardonnay and Sauvignon Blanc being lighter bodied, having no tannins, and having more subtle natural flavors and aromas to begin with, oak usage can be more readily perceived when the wines are smelled and tasted. Thus, there is more intense nuttiness and spice present in white wines aged in oak versus red wines.

Many people struggle with identifying oak in wine. They want to know the best ways to identify it in their wine. My best tip is to go to your local wine store and ask for a heavily oaked wine and a completely unoaked wine. Do this for both reds and whites, and compare them. As noted, the wines with oak have the added aromatics and mouthfeel of vanilla, toast, and spice. The unoaked wines will have a fresher and purer character overall.

Once you have the clear comparison, your understanding of oak and its relation to a finished wine will grow immensely. Also, putting comparisons into practice will make for one heck of a wine night.

What does oxygen do to wine?

Oxygen can have several roles when it comes to wine. Much like everything in life, a little can be beneficial, but too much can ruin everything. As we know, a giant premise behind oak involves subtly introducing wine to oxygen, but there are even more extreme examples of oxygen's role in wine. Let's look at both ends of the spectrum to nail down oxygen's role in wine.

Beaujolais and Oloroso sherry are two great examples of the differing winemaking objectives concerning oxygen.

Beaujolais is a region in southern Burgundy. The main grape here is Gamay. A signature style of the region is to produce wines with a fresh, fruity, and vibrant style. To achieve this, they make two specific choices. They protect the grape *must* (the grapes that will be fermented) from oxygen before and during fermentation. They do what's called carbonic maceration: they dump the uncrushed grapes into a large tank, and then blanket them with carbon dioxide and close the top to protect the grapes from oxygen.

By doing this, the grapes explode from the inside out, releasing juice, and begin fermentation in this way instead of being pressed mechanically. After fermentation is complete, winemakers don't put the wine in barrels to age at all. They let the finished wine settle in steel tanks and bottle it shortly after. When fermenting in this way, the resulting wine is extremely fruity, bright, and lifted because oxygen doesn't play a role in the production.

Oloroso sherry is an entirely different story. Sherry could warrant a whole book on its own, but here's the gist. Opposed to the Gamay from Beaujolais, a lot of a sherry's taste and character comes from purposeful exposure to oxygen during the aging process. Also, *oloroso* is a term that lets the drinker know what the style of wine will be. By aging the wine for years in an oxidative environment, nutty, caramel-like, and more robust, developed flavors are achieved.

Many of the wines we enjoy day to day have a "normal" relationship with oxygen. Thus, wines aren't intentionally isolated from oxygen or encouraged to change due to oxygen exposure. A normally produced Pinot Noir is a fantastic example to contrast with a Gamay produced using carbonic maceration. The Pinot Noir will have a less bright, fruity, lifted nature to it compared to the Gamay. Instead, the slight exposure to oxygen in the winemaking process (especially if aged in an oak barrel) makes the Pinot Noir richer, smoother, and more dimensional.

5

A Sea of Grapes

AFTER DAYS OF TRAVELING AND REMINISCING, I finally saw the road sign displaying fifty-six miles to Napa. Fifty-six miles until I laid eyes on the place I had been envisioning in my mind but had never seen in person. Only stories from my parents and books had given me clues about what to expect. During some down time while traveling in Europe, I had skimmed books about the valley. I read about its rise from a sleepy pastoral town in the early 1900s to the wine destination it transformed into. I discovered the evolution of Napa all had to do with forward-thinking winemakers thrusting their wines onto the global stage.

In the late 1970s, a few ambitious producers put their wines up against the famous wines of Europe in a competition called The Judgement of Paris. Two wines from Napa took home first place in both the white and red categories, beating out the French. After Napa Valley earned those awards and international respect, it exploded with winery development and visitors from around the world. In the years following, Napa continued to craft wines and a lifestyle people marveled at.

Much like Napa's rise to wine mecca, I felt like I was on the precipice of something extraordinary. Then a thought flashed into my head. What if it wasn't what I expected? I had never been there before, and I had based my expectations on only my parents' vivid memories of the place and books. What if it wasn't for me? All the time and effort, and I could be going into something incapable of making me happy.

Those kinds of dark thoughts had a way of creeping into my mind. I briefly flashed back to standing in my college apartment kitchen and being called a nobody. I worked to rid the doubt from my mind in favor of making Napa everything I imagined, no matter what.

We pulled into the River Terrace Inn smack in the middle of downtown Napa. I continued to search for the emotion I longed for the place to give me as my mom put the car into park. I thought the downtown district was charming, although a faint clawing feeling of lackluster crept back in. It was perfectly pleasant enough and all, but I didn't seem quite like the mecca I had been searching for. I put the thoughts aside to focus on getting my mom and myself settled at the hotel before searching for a place for me to live.

We didn't have time even to take a breather, because I had managed to set up a few prospective house appointments. I had searched Craigslist for a good portion of the trip, trying to find somewhere to live. The most affordable option for me was a room in a house. I certainly didn't take the Inglenook job for the paycheck.

The first option was in the city center of Napa, not five minutes from the hotel. We pulled up to a cute little bungalow, and the landlord showed us around. He was renting out two rooms. The month's rent far exceeded my meager budget, but my parents were adamant about helping me get my footing and had offered to help make ends meet. I had vowed to repay them for giving me the gift of stability, which could seem like a freebie for some "entitled" girl to the outside world.

The landlord waited exactly two minutes after showing me the bungalow before asking aloud how much I was going to make at my job. I revealed my hourly wage. With a smug look, he assured me I would never be able to afford it. I was mortified. I hadn't even started my job, and someone had already implied I was somewhat pitiful.

My mom came to defense, interjecting that she and my father would be helping with part of the rent. His tune changed and he immediately ignored me to talk numbers with my mom. As we walked to the car with the lease application, my mom and I glanced at each other to say there was no way we were giving money to that ass.

With thoughts of money, status, and judging eyes still swirling around my head, we sped off to view a condo option in the opposite part of downtown. I couldn't shake the feeling of belittlement from the harsh landlord. I asked my mom if she was proud of me regardless of what my paycheck might be. She assured me she was prouder of me than I could've imagined. She told me following my heart and wanting to create something extraordinary with my life made her and my dad infinitely proud.

Just as my heart was swelling, we turned into the apartment complex. After pulling into a parking spot, we lingered and took in our surroundings. In the five minutes sitting idle, not saying a word, three white-haired women walked by with three little fluffy white dogs. We caught the tail end of what looked like an old folks' shuffleboard match. The silence continued.

Without saying a word, my mom started the engine and slowly pulled out of the apartment complex. All I could manage to say was, "They didn't advertise it as an older person's home in the Craigslist ad." We both burst out laughing.

The sun was setting as we traveled to the third and final option for the day. We were both wearing slightly forced smiles as the chances of finding me a home looked bleak. We headed away from downtown to check out the next home. It was a room in a house for rent. Craigslist advertised it as a "wine country" home. I couldn't resist the thought of living among the vines, but my skepticism of Craigslist ads had grown immensely after the retirement community mishap.

We drove farther and farther away from downtown. As we made a left turn down an isolated road, I lost my breath. Finally, the sight I had longed for since the moment Helen told me the job was mine. Lush, verdant vineyards appeared before my eyes. The sky was a hundred shades of pink, purple, and blue. At that moment everything felt right.

My eyes were transfixed on the surreal appearance of my surroundings. The vineyard-lined road and indescribable beauty led us
to a white two-story home nestled among the vines.

I gazed at the house and embraced the thought that everything
that day had guided me there. The only hang-up could be a crazy
person residing in the storybook home. I knocked and hoped for
some sense of normalcy. I took a deep breath as the doorknob turned.

A seemingly run-of-the-mill man answered. My relief at finding
an ordinary person on the other side was countered by my mom's
apprehensive expression. Regardless of my mom's initial objection to
me living in the same home as a man, he ushered us in.

He gave us the full tour of this five-bedroom home and spoke of
the other tenants, a couple, living there. They were organic farmers,
and he was a barrel maker. It couldn't have gotten more "Napa" than
that. At the end of the tour, he said I would be more than welcome
to rent out a room.

We took the rental papers and headed out to the car, and I knew
I was home. My first real home in the "real world" seemed about as

far away from the real world as you could get. I would be living in a sea of grapes.

With housing much more under control, my mom and I both felt a huge relief. She had wanted to stay for a week to get me all settled. I was set to start my job five days from when we arrived, so we had some time to explore the valley. My mom wanted to show me how she fell in love with this place. We hopped in the car with a more carefree air and drove away from the city center and to the heart of the valley.

Row after row of vines continued to capture my mind, as they had the evening before. As we took a turn from a back road and hit the main drag that went straight through the valley, what I saw made everything worth it. The job hunt, packing up my whole life, driving across the country, and the stress of finding a new home all faded from my mind. All I saw and felt was the heart of the place. Maybe it was because I knew it would be mine for a time, but I had never seen anything more beautiful.

As we drove along this main road, majestic mountain ranges rose up on both sides, the vines were a vivid green, the sky was so richly blue it seemed hard to believe, and it was as if there actually could be a heaven on earth. Then a sign appeared before us: welcome to world-famous wine-growing region, napa valley, and a quote read, "The wine is bottled poetry."

Oh, how I wanted to experience its poetry. I didn't want to just drink wine. I wanted to discover what the man who called it bottled poetry found in his glass. After twenty more minutes of driving with my heart pounding, we came upon what looked like small-town USA. The town was called St. Helena. I fell silent. My mom looked over as though to try to figure out what I was thinking. I looked back at her through watery eyes and told her it was all more than I had imagined.

Napa had stunned me with its breathtaking scenery. The thing was, a great view means pretty much nothing unless there is someone to share it with. I still had my mom, but finding friends in the quaint Napa Valley started seeming somewhat difficult. It's not like I lived in a college town full of young people anymore.

The morning of my third day in Napa, my mom burst into our hotel room. She exclaimed she had found me a friend. True to form, as she always wanted to make sure I was going to be okay. Meeting new people was one of my favorite things, and the fact that my mom had screened my potential first friend in Napa didn't bother me one bit.

My mom gave me all the details. She had been talking to someone at the front desk when she met Katie. She said she was around my age and used the term "good egg" in describing her. Well, I couldn't argue with that. So, next thing I know, we're heading down to the front desk to meet Katie.

As we approached the front desk, two young girls were checking people in. We waited for the line in front of us to dwindle. I watched each girl interact with the people. The one on the right seemed to be a bit superficial, and I didn't get a warm or inviting vibe from her at all. The girl on the left seemed lively and had a much more pleasant energy.

As we were next in line, I was thinking, *Please let Katie be the girl on the left. Please.* Then my mom said, "And this is Katie."

The girl on the left looked up and smiled.

We hit it off immediately, and I knew my mom was relieved that she wouldn't truly be leaving me alone.

There are a lot of monumental firsts in life. Your first day of school, your first sporting event, your first recital, or your first day at your grown-up job. What these days all have in common is that you want someone cheering you on. For me, the day had finally come. It wasn't like every other part-time job or internship I'd had. I couldn't tell if I was nervous, excited, or just scared. It felt right for my mom to be there on that first day. She hugged me and wished me luck.

I jumped in the car and made my way to Inglenook. My mom and I had rehearsed the ride earlier in the week, so at least I knew I wouldn't get lost finding it. The same feelings filled my heart driving through the valley as the days before. I drove by winery after winery and then finally spotted the Inglenook sign.

I raced down the long driveway. The winery grew larger and grander as I drew nearer. The château (fancy name for winery) was like something out of a movie. Actually, that made perfect sense because, as I recalled, Francis Ford Coppola was the current owner. *Stunning* wasn't the right word; *majestic* suited it far better.

Still in a trance, I pulled my car into a spot and turned off the ignition. I paused for a moment, still not quite knowing what I was doing or what I was about to walk into. I had journeyed such a long way for the moment standing before me. I turned the door handle and stepped out. The parking lot was quite a way from the main building, and I was considerably slow from taking it all in.

Everywhere I looked something caught my attention. The view back to the main road was pristine vine after pristine vine. The walk to the château was bordered by manicured gardens, pergolas, and a grand fountain. Yet again, it almost didn't feel real.

I flashed back into reality when I realized my pace was setting me behind. Last thing I needed was to be late on my first day. I reached the majestic main entrance. Of course the door looked like a door from an imposing castle and was locked. I knocked aggressively, and finally my frantic banging was met with a woman in all black ushering me in.

She was friendly enough, and I would later learn her name was Reyna. As I stepped into the magnificent structure, I was slightly confused. It was nothing like what I imagined a "winery" being. This looked more like an ornate palace of sorts. Regardless, I needed to find the woman who interviewed me weeks previously. There was absolutely no one around.

As I searched for Jenna, I spotted a brown-haired profession-al-looking woman scurrying down the stairs. She greeted me, and I apologized for my tardiness as she led me up the stairs. Walking up the grandiose staircase, she commented on some of the château's historical significance. Then, midsentence, she asked if I was wearing perfume.

I answered yes and was about to share the brand when she said, "You can't wear that."

I wasn't sure what exactly I would be doing that would prohibit any perfume. She merely stated, "It distracts from the aroma of the wine." Great, now she knew I was an absolute novice. I assured her I would only work with my natural aroma going forward. She cracked a small smile and opened the door to the third-floor office.

Meeting everyone in the office was a blur. Next thing I knew, I was sitting in her private office talking through all the job details. She let me know that David G. was my supervisor and that I would report to him. Then she told me more about my position. I obviously knew the broad role I would assume as a bistro associate, but I didn't know many of the specifics.

She made it clear it was a seasonal position with a chance to be hired full time after the summer season. It was a huge "small" detail I'd read in the small print of the application but somehow pushed from my mind upon taking the job. She proceeded to tell me David would be training me on the day-to-day tasks of a bistro associate. The job description on the application had left it all quite vague. However, I knew I would be at a winery every day with a chance to learn about wine and be with people. I believed the rest would fall into place.

Then she got to my outfit. Helen had emailed me during the drive out to California that my uniform would be a white button-down and black pants. Wanting to make a fabulous impression, I was wearing a stylish white shirt and black business pants. I wanted to pour wine looking distinguished and chic, of course. My stylish bubble was burst as Jenna went on to say I would need a different outfit for the bistro tasks. I thought, *What the hell will I be doing besides pouring a few tastes of wine?*

She whisked me away to a "uniform closet" and pulled out a man's white button-down, the style of which you might find on an Olive Garden server, and a pair of black slacks (much less flattering than my current pants). With my hands full of the clothing I wasn't thrilled about having to wear, I turned the corner to see David.

As he extended his hand to introduce himself, he had an automatic warmth about him. He let me know I would be with him for the day and promised to take me through everything and turn me into a pro. He put me at ease. I wanted to take in everything he could teach me about Inglenook.

David and I headed down to the bistro. As we walked down from the offices, we went further into the heart of the building. He guided me through the long caves lined with barrels, the impressive cellar, and the pristine shop filled with the finest keepsakes imported from Italy and France. It was unlike any "winery" I had conjured up in my mind. The tour ended with the area they called the bistro. I stepped into the room, and it looked like an authentic café straight out of France.

As soon as I walked in, I was overcome by an intoxicating smell of espresso, wine, and the historic mustiness of the château. The smell had a way of drawing me in and making me feel at home in the new space. David looked around himself with an air of pride, and I knew this place meant a lot to him.

We headed to the counter, which he said would be my office. To my right were old-fashioned barn doors that slid open to reveal a view of the pristine courtyard and never-ending vineyards beyond. Although it wasn't an advertising office in a big city, I thrilled to call the bistro my "office."

He began taking me through what my actual responsibilities would be. And while the whole "pouring wine" thing was included in my agenda, it certainly wasn't my main task. The most unexpected realization was that I would be a literal barista. Not only would I be making coffee drinks, but I would be in charge of making cheese plates for the tastings, taking empty bottles out to the garbage, making huge batches of lemon granita weekly, receiving and unloading dozens of cartons of milk, keeping everything stocked and tidy, washing dishes, and of course serving wines by the glass along with food offerings. As David outlined task after task, suspicion crept into my head. I began to feel like Inglenook could've hired any random person for this position.

I started removing my rose-colored glasses. It hit me that I was using my college degree to make coffee and pour wines by the glass, among other less glamorous tasks. I was close to thinking I had just made the worst decision of my life. When David handed me the bistro manual of opening and closing procedures, I could feel my face sinking. We said our goodbyes, and I was scheduled to come in for training the next day. Slightly defeated, I walked away from the château and was greeted by the glorious Napa sunshine. Driving away from the château, its grandiose nature had the power to start shaking the feelings of doubt from my mind.

I decided right then and there I was going to be the best bistro associate that place had ever seen. I may have been the bottom of the totem pole, but I wasn't going to stay there. I would use every opportunity to learn more about wine and make something happen.

Something my dad told me once kept ringing in my ears. He told me that he didn't care what my career was in life. He said it only mattered that, whatever I did, I gave it everything I had and that I was the absolute best at it I could be. I took one last look at Inglenook before turning onto the main road, promising myself I would find a way to make the experience extraordinary.

I pulled into the River Terrace Inn, and my mom was waiting in the lobby to greet me. All her questions filled my already spinning head. I exceled at extracting every possible positive thing while downplaying the negatives. I regaled her with all the glamorous details of the château and grounds. I told her they were starting me in the bistro to pour and gain more experience with wine. I left out the uniform change and the fact that I was essentially a waitress-barista hybrid. Instead, I focused on how much I was going to learn and how I could grow there. I had to make sure she wasn't scared for me. I couldn't live with myself if she was worrying about my future from thousands of miles away.

Let's just say, the fact that it was meant to be a six-month seasonal position remained something I purposefully left out. That was for me to worry about. She took me out to celebrate my first day. On her last night with me, we sat on a rooftop in downtown Napa sipping wine. It was another storybook night where the sky went from blue to pink and purple to finally a light periwinkle.

I watched my mom as she gazed out on the valley. Her eyes at that moment reminded me of all the times she would tell me about this place back in Florida. We continued to revel in the moment. After a few more sips of Chardonnay, the realization of my mom flying thousands of miles away the next morning put a pit in my stomach. Regardless of the sudden reality check I was wrestling with, I relished that we had done everything we set out to do.

We drove across the country, found me a safe place to live in a day, shared in the magic of the valley, created connections with people, and successfully proved even the most unlikely of dreams had a chance at coming true.

Wine Talk: Old-World Versus New-World Wines

Comparing wines from the Old World and the New World is one of my favorite wine activities. I marvel at how the same grape grown in Europe versus in the US can taste so dramatically different. The comparison exercise is a testament to the diversity and depth of wine.

When reflecting on the subject of old-world wines, I recall when I first tasted wines from France, Italy, and Spain. I tried the wines of Europe during my postgraduation backpacking trip. It was during that trip I started noticing slight differences in the wines I tasted compared to the wines of California I was used to. I observed them changing with the delicacies we indulged in. They smelled and tasted so unfamiliar, and I couldn't put into words what I was experiencing.

However, the first useful lessons I learned concerning the wines of Europe were far more valuable to me than what I could've read in a book. I discovered red wine from France tasted incredible in front of the Eiffel Tower and enticed me to smoke a cigarette. I found out a glass of Italian white wine could be discussed in poetic terms when a passionate Italian sommelier discovered my fascination. I realized a Spanish wine had even more soul when watching the sun set from a mountaintop.

I left Europe with my first true insights about wine from different places. Wine was the ultimate connector—it connects people, places, and cultures. And not only does it create connections, but wine can act as the vehicle to take you back to distinctive moments in time. In this way, tasting old-world versus new-world wines should become intuitive. Being able to feel and appreciate the differences of old-world and new-world wines helps to unravel wine's mystery.

What makes a wine *new-world* versus *old-world*?
Describing a wine as being either a new-world wine or an old-world wine refers to the specific geographic location a wine comes from. If someone refers to a wine as *new-world*, they are implying that the grapes used to make the wine were grown in an area other than Europe. Some main new-world countries to know are the United States, Australia, New Zealand, South Africa, and Argentina. If you are drinking a wine from any of these places, it's classified as new-world. Conversely, if you're drinking a wine made from grapes grown in Europe, it's an old-world wine.

Now, where things get interesting is how the style of wine changes from Old to New World. There are some general guidelines to help you distinguish between old-world and new-world wines. New-world wines tend to be more polished and fruit-driven and taste very similar to how they smell. Old-world wines tend to be more rustic and earthy and have a different taste than what one might expect from the smell. These nuances come about because of the differing climates, soils types, vine ages, vineyard management, winemaking traditions, and overall respective characteristics.

Why do wines from the New World smell "sweeter" than those from the Old World?

The word *sweet* is commonly misused when it comes to wine. A lot of people use the word *sweet* when talking about a wine's smells when they really mean "ripe" or "intense." When you smell aromas that are sweet in your mind, try to think about what you are smelling to make them appear that way. You aren't smelling actual sugar, but perhaps more intense fruit leading you to believe its sugar. Riper fruit and "sweeter" smells are associated with wines from warmer climates or wines that have been aged in oak barrels. The toasted inside of the oak barrel touching the wine for a number of months or years incorporates lactones into the wine, giving it the tastes and aromas of vanilla, baking spices, and butterscotch. New wines typically smell "sweeter" because of the warmer climates (riper fruit smell) on average and more liberal use of new oak.

As previously mentioned, old-world wines don't share new-world's ripeness, polish, and generous oak usage. The result is a wine that doesn't smell as "sweet." Rather, the wines have more "funky" aromas. These funky aromas result from letting the grapes and the places they are grown shine through more. The aromas more common in wines from the Old World are less ripe fruits with a greater presence of herbs/flowers/spices, more minerality, and subtler oak character.

What should I expect from new-world versus old-world wines, and why?
Simple things to look for are a greater presence of fruit, a more polished style, and a less obvious mineral/earthy presence. The mineral presence in wines just means there are tastes and smells making us think of rocks, chalk, dirt, or the forest floor. Smelling an overwhelming amount of these will most likely point to an old-world wine.

A lot of people wonder *why* this is. It all comes down to the age of the vine, the climate where the vine is grown, soil types, and how the producer chooses to treat the vine and craft the wine. Thus, you can look for a more perfumed aroma, polished taste, and more approachable quality. We are making some general assumptions, but these guidelines will help you wrap your head around the difference between the two.

For example, if you have a Cabernet Sauvignon from Napa—a new-world wine—you can expect ripe blackberries, black cherries, black currants, fresh leather, anise, cinnamon, vanilla, and a caramelized aroma on the nose. When you drink a wine like this from the New World, it will have a polished, smooth feel with all the ripe fruit and oak usage enveloping your whole palate. The wine will have a strong presence, but still be easy to drink, with a long, warming finish.

In general, old-world wines will transform more dramatically during a meal. Say you have a Cabernet Sauvignon from Bordeaux, which will typically include a blend of Merlot, Cabernet Franc, and Petit Verdot grapes. You will notice more underripe black currants, black currant leaf, blackberries, green pepper, cigar box, dried violets, musty aromas, turned earth, subtle vanilla from oak, and a mineral, earth-driven nature on the nose. When you taste this wine, you can expect a more unrounded and unpolished feel on your palate. The flavors you experience will be more of the earthy, and the wine will finish with less alcoholic warmth. The old-world Bordeaux Cabernet Sauvignon–based wine presents an opportunity to discover how a wine can evolve with food.

Why do professionals seem to value old-world wines more than new-world wines?

A lot of people interested in wine believe a wine is only "high quality" if it's made in Europe. Wine connoisseurs of the past believed only European wines reflected traditions and expertise in winemaking. The new-world winemaking regions were seen as somewhat of a joke in the greater world of wine. Some believed the vineyards of California, Australia, and South Africa couldn't compete with those of France, Italy, and Spain. However, as minds opened and new-world regions improved their craft, perceptions began to change.

In a broader sense, quality comes from how well the grapes are grown, the expertise going into the winemaking, and the overall balance in the wine. The styles will be different between old-world and new-world wines, but that doesn't necessarily mean one will always be better than the other. Don't box yourself in by only seeing the beauty in wines from Burgundy, Bordeaux, Barolo, and Champagne.

What are some other new-world wines to check out other than those from California?

The New World is literally every other wine-producing region other than Europe. Explore it! My favorite new-world wine-producing country is Australia. There is far more to the wine regions of Australia than has historically been understood. Australia is so much more than Yellow Tail. Try a Chardonnay from Adelaide Hills by Shaw and Smith, a Cabernet Sauvignon by Leeuwin Estate from Margaret River, or a sparkling wine by Jansz from Tasmania.

It can be very exciting to sample wines from developing winemaking regions in the New World. These regions can often be more approachable and affordable than time-tested old-world regions. One such example is Uruguay. There are many stunning wines coming out of that country. Try a producer called Bodegas Garzon and their wine made from the Tannat grape.

New York State is also producing countless delicious and complex wines. Try a producer called Hermann J. Wiemer and their Riesling.

New Zealand is making diverse and high-quality wines as well. They are so much more than just Sauvignon Blanc. The Pinot Noirs from New Zealand are a great way to get a taste of the largely undiscovered red wines of New Zealand. Go for one from Central Otago by a producer called Craggy Range.

It's a big, beautiful wine world out there, with quality to be discovered from every region. An open mind can make drinking wine all the more exciting. Instead of being fenced in by an outdated view on quality wine, there can be value in distinguishing high-quality up-and-coming wine regions in the New World. For instance, New York State, Washington State, and Argentina are making noteworthy strides in quality and wine expression.

6

The Napa Lifestyle

THE MOMENT I WATCHED MY MOM roll her suitcase into SFO airport felt like time standing still. As she faded out of sight, I finally realized everyone who cared about me would be thousands of miles of away. Moreover, I had promised everyone I was going to do something special in California. The uncertainty of it all chipped away at the sunny disposition I had maintained through all my recent life-altering changes. As I sat in my car with the engine running, I knew my mom wasn't going to turn around and save me from my doubt. For one of the first times, my safety net was gone.

What I did realize at that moment was sitting in a parked car wasn't good for anything. I resolved that the only way to see the sunshine was to keep looking up. So I tore my eyes away from the airport doors and set my gaze on San Francisco and beyond. I roamed around the city all day. I did every touristy thing I could think of. I listened to the barking seals, climbed huge hills, explored Chinatown, snapped photos of the *Full House* home, and drove down the iconic zigzag hill. I relished in the same sensations Europe had brought me a month earlier. As I was eating an authentic Chinese dessert, the fact that it was three thirty in the afternoon hit me.

My mom's last piece of motherly advice was to make sure and leave the city before three thirty to avoid outrageous traffic. I assumed she had been exaggerating about the traffic nightmare. I was at my car by four o'clock and threw the top down, ready to feel the wind in my hair during the hour-and-a-half drive back to wine country. Within five minutes of traveling through the city streets, I hit a standstill. My mom was right, yet again. Between getting out of the city and driving back to Napa, a one-and-a-half-hour trip turned into four hours.

When I finally arrived in Napa, I was famished. I headed to the place that reminded me of home, Whole Foods. Looking for the food bar, I heard someone calling my name. In my mind, it seemed completely impossible since I didn't know more than six people in the entire valley. I turned to see a smiling face staring back at me. It was one of my new roommates, Emily. She and her boyfriend Alex had the room down the hall from me. They were organic farmers, and I had only briefly met them as I was moving in.

She told me she was making dinner for everyone later in the evening and I had to join. Despite my exhaustion, I had the feeling I needed to be there. We spent that evening devouring vegetables from their organic garden and other homemade dishes Alex whipped up.

I didn't have a chance to think about my apprehensions, and the couple had their chance to ask me the obvious question. It was a question I would get again and again during my first few months in California. They wanted to know how the heck a twentysomething from Florida, with no wine experience and without so much as a visit to California under her belt, ended up in Napa Valley. I told them my story and watched their eyes grow wider. Saying it all aloud helped reaffirm it was the path I was meant to be on.

During the dinner, I heard all about what it was like to live in Napa from my new friends. My perceptions started shifting as I received a window into their lives. Most importantly, I felt like I could create a life there.

High off the fact I had a stable and friendly living situation, I made my way confidently to Inglenook the next morning. It was my official first day. I had my "server" uniform on and an unshakable desire to blow everyone away. I hadn't met my coworkers yet since I had consistently trained during off hours, and I didn't really know what to expect.

I had misjudged my commute and was running a few minutes behind. I rushed toward the winery, not wanting to make a bad impression on my first official day. Even in my haste, I gawked at the château. I passed through the grand entrance door and rushed through the caves of the historic building toward the bistro. I could hear the morning meeting already in progress, so I waited at the side entrance so as not to distract the group.

My supervisor, David, led the meeting and, upon seeing me rush in, announced he wanted to introduce the brand-new bistro associate to everyone. I half waved to everyone and glanced around the room. As I searched for an open seat, a thought dawned on me. The fifteen or so men and women I observed were mostly middle-aged. There wasn't anyone even remotely close to my age. I was concerned that I wouldn't be able to relate to my coworkers and wondered if this would be a good fit for me. There weren't even that many women. Did I just insert myself into some good old boys' wine club?

As I sat down, I racked my brain trying to recall all the opening duties for the bistro. As I mentally went through the training manual, an older man with a big, bushy mustache leaned over and introduced himself as Harold. He had a palpable warmth about him and a Cheshire Cat smile. He exclaimed he was thrilled to work together and if I needed anything, he was the guy to ask. He told me he had been the Château Ambassador for almost fifteen years.

The woman on my other side leaned over as well. She introduced herself as Nancy. From the moment we met, I knew she would be my "work mom." She had a calmness about her that made me feel very at ease. I genuinely felt that she wanted to help me out as I was the "newbie." They weren't all exactly what I expected, but I felt they were all going to be characters with good hearts. With that, David ended the meeting and I sprang up ready to get to work.

Everyone sauntered to their various roles in the winery, and a gentleman named Ed stayed behind to help me on my first day in the bistro. He was retired and had essentially got a job pouring wine at Inglenook for fun. Somehow the almost retiree and I got along seamlessly. He was the coolest "older" guy I had ever met. He told me the real details about Inglenook and what all to expect from day-to-day life there. With him, I received all the insider information, and I couldn't get enough.

As he revealed more and more about my new workplace, I discovered I knew very little about it. One particular fact struck me. Francis Ford Coppola owned Inglenook and lived behind the property in a historic home built by the original founder in the 1800s. Francis Ford Coppola was a director with the same fame level of Stephen Spielberg and James Cameron.

I remembered my first time watching a film Francis directed, *The Godfather*. The movie moved me with its storytelling and intrigue. I recalled seeing "Directed by Francis Ford Coppola" flash up first in the credits and thinking the man must have been a genius.

In terms of Inglenook, I was convinced he would be like the Easter Bunny or Santa Claus: I assumed he would be more myth, rather than hanging around the château. Still, being able to say I *technically* worked for Francis Ford Coppola impressed me, at least.

As my curiosity about Inglenook grew, I noticed the general curiosity in my story did as well. Coworker after coworker wanted to know what brought me there. Even guests grabbing a glass of wine or a latte wanted to know my tale. I suppose a young woman slinging wine and crafting cappuccinos inspired questions.

Sometimes, before I could even open my mouth, people would try to answer the question for me. They all assumed I had traveled thousands of miles because I'd followed a man there. I experienced the greatest satisfaction being able to say I decided to move to Napa for me. I never did feed into the delusion that I needed a man by my side to have worth.

I became skilled at turning my story into a highlight reel. Otherwise, the bistro line would start backing up as I tried to communicate what brought me to Inglenook. Even with my condensed version, I witnessed people's eyes light up when I would share my personal journey with them. I wanted to believe my experience of following my passion against all odds had a minuscule effect on them. I wished that at least one person would do something that he or she had always deemed impossible after I shared my stories in the bistro.

My second day on the job, my coworkers' faces became less of a blur. I tried to get everyone's name right. I failed. Everyone was patient with me, despite my repeated "What was your name again?" I wanted to both learn more about the people I would be spending so much time with and see where I stacked up with my wine knowledge.

My second day I partook in my first formal tasting. I figured I would learn more about wine but felt confident I had the wine skills to keep up with everyone. I was the "wine girl" in college after all, and I convinced myself I knew what I was talking about. David led the tasting and poured everyone a hearty sample of a rich red wine. I assumed it was a Cabernet Sauvignon.

He told us the red wine was the new release of Inglenook's estate Zinfandel. I looked down at my red wine and thought he must have had a slip of the tongue. The only Zinfandel I had ever tasted was a blush color and came out of a box. I figured he must have said the wrong grape and raised my hand to achieve some clarification.

David nodded for me to ask my question. I asked if he'd meant to call the wine Zinfandel. Looking slightly puzzled, he told me, once again, it was Zinfandel and wanted to know where my confusion was coming from.

I answered back, "If it's Zinfandel, why is it red?" I figured it was a question everyone else was thinking too.

A smirk appeared on his face. He let me know Zinfandel was a red grape and made red wine. He indicated that my confusion was that a rosé-style wine could be made from the grape and was generally referred to as *white zin*.

I could feel what everyone in the room was thinking: that I had absolutely no wine knowledge. My embarrassment hit its peak, and I knew I would have to work twice as hard as everyone else just to have a base knowledge of wine. This situation didn't make me resent or fear wine—it made me desire to know it more.

After the tasting, I was back to the more menial tasks requiring no wine knowledge. I was wiping down the tables in the courtyard when a four-wheeler zoomed toward me. I assumed it was a vineyard worker tending to the vines. I was standing by a metal chain that blocked off the access up a hill leading to the vineyards at the back of the property and the owner's home. The man on the four-wheeler came closer and closer, and I strained my eyes to see a somewhat older gentleman. For a brief second, I thought the vineyard worker looked a lot like Francis Ford Coppola. However, there was no way a world-famous director would be speeding toward me on a four-wheeler.

The mysterious man continued barreling toward me. The driver came to a screeching halt three feet in front of me. As I hopped back a few inches, it dawned on me—I was standing three feet away from the legendary Coppola. I had only seen pictures of him. I stood entranced, and I didn't dare speak.

He stared at me with the engine idling. He looked at the chain and then he looked at me. We were silent for a few seconds. He asked if I could help him out, looking at the chain. I rushed to remove the chain, and I held it as he began to putter up the hill.

Slowing almost to a stop as he went by, he looked me up and down and said, "You are new here, huh?"

My mouth stopped working. Just as he was about to completely pass by me, I managed to say, "Yes. I'm from Florida." Like Francis Ford Coppola cared where I was from.

He glanced over his shoulder and said, "Welcome to heaven," and told me he would see me around.

I put the chain back into place, and he vanished into the vineyards.

I regaled the lunch table with my Francis story the next day. I was at least making somewhat of a name for myself among my coworkers. I also learned lesson number one of Inglenook: I would never be bored.

I spent a month in California. The magic of the place only gained intensity with each passing day. In my short time there, the unpredictable nature of my days continued to gain steam. For instance, a guest at Inglenook asked me to model for her in a fashion show hosted at a local winery, I witnessed a hot air balloon land outside my bedroom window, and I started meeting the most interesting people in unexpected ways.

One particular friend was Jassy. She had been the only other "model" under thirty-five at the fashion show I was randomly asked to participate in. Another was named Manny. He happened to be an assistant to the designer who had requested me to wear her clothing in the show.

I had three solid people, including Katie from the front desk at River Terrace, I could make dinners with, grab coffee with, and call my friends. Having people to enjoy life with always meant a lot to me. They had nothing to do with wine and couldn't progress my career, but to me, that was never a reason to befriend someone. I learned as I ventured out into "the real world," these motives found a way of influencing friendship decisions.

Despite making connections in Napa, I was still struggling to find my identity at Inglenook. I'm sure people only saw me as a temporary fixture in the scope of things. True to my character, I longed for more than just surface-level relationships. My opportunity came when I was invited to one of the wine club manager's house-warming parties, and I would have a chance to see everyone outside of work. The night of the party arrived, and it ended up being mostly small talk. There wasn't quite the turnout I was hoping for either. I left the party feeling somewhat deflated. I knew I would make a "work" family eventually, but when and how remained to be seen.

Regardless of my thoughts about the evening, I crawled into my bed after the party and vivid dreams ensued. I mostly dreamed about everything that had happened to me over the last few weeks. It was amazing how lifelike the people, the vines, and Inglenook were as they danced across my mind. Then my dream took on a whole different dimension. Everything started shaking inside my head. I thought it was the most violent dream I had ever experienced. Reality hit me like a freight train as I felt my eyelids snap open. My dream turned out to be real.

Everything was falling off the shelves in my room, and the whole house was rocking back and forth. I froze, watching picture frames, books, and flower vases all come crashing down around me. I couldn't comprehend the immediate and intense disorientation. My hands clutched my sheets for what felt like twenty minutes after the house stopped shaking.

I surveyed the destruction all around me and waited to wake up again from the nightmare. Instead, there was a moment of complete and utter silence. It was a bone-chilling silence—as though everyone in Napa Valley was thinking the very same thoughts and completely paralyzed. The silence quickly turned to a symphony of sirens, alarms, and dogs barking. After all was said and done, I had been rocked by the largest and most destructive earthquake Napa had seen in at least fifty years.

Welcome to California, Kara.

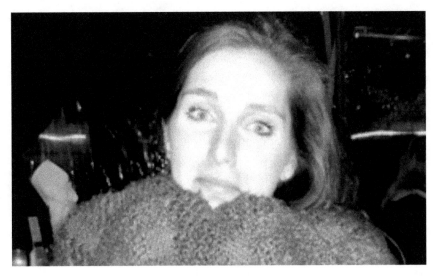

Wine Talk: All Things Service and Storage

When I was first working the bistro, I spent several hours unloading wine into a cellar for proper storage every week. As I lifted bottle after bottle into place, I began questioning why it was necessary to go to all the trouble. First of all, I didn't know why aging wine was so important. I wanted to know the reasons for all my manual labor. My coworkers shed light on the fact that wine needed very specific characteristics to age correctly. Through my efforts to rest the wines on their sides, in a fifty-five-degree cellar, safe from sunlight, I was helping set the wines up for aging success.

Moreover, my time in the bistro created a new perspective for me concerning wine presentation and service. Before my Californian wine adventure, I had never thought about wine as being alive or changing, based on the different ways it was served. However, my first few days in Napa Valley showed me just how significant the service and storage of wine were. I had mostly enjoyed wine in plastic cups in college. It was a rare occasion when I was able to indulge with a proper glass. But now, in the bistro, I had several different sizes of glasses and very specific ways to open and pour wine.

After some time, I didn't fumble with opening wine bottles, I poured the wine elegantly into the correct glasses, and I knew just the amount of wine equal to a five-ounce glass. Even more importantly, I started to understand the rhyme and reason to all the energy put into handling wine properly. When wine is stored and served the proper way, the whole experience changes. Remembering and utilizing a few simple service and storage practices can bring even more enjoyment to your next wine night.

What temperature do I serve white wines? Are ice cubes allowed?
Let's get real: no one has a thermometer on them at all times. I don't

even like to give general temperature ranges, because they aren't practical. So, an easy-to-follow rule is to serve whites at slightly warmer than refrigerator temperature.

Thus, pull a white from your refrigerator and then open and serve it after five minutes. By doing this, you will assure the wine won't be too warm or too cold. A mistake many people make when serving whites is serving them too cold. When whites are served too cold, they start to lose their nuances of aroma, flavor, and structure. Letting the wine warm up ever so slightly allows more of the wine's character to show through.

Now: ice cubes. A request for ice in a white, a rosé, or even a red can make any sommelier cringe. The reason we can be "snobs" about it is because ice will drastically change the chemical makeup and character of the wine. It's simply not the way the winemaker intended the wine to be. Ice will dilute the subtle nuance and character of the wine.

However, I can only guide someone to water, I can't make them drink. If someone asks for ice, I'm not going to spit in their face. My job is to make sure every second of the wine-drinking experience is sensational. If someone craves a more intimate knowledge of wine, I am there. If someone is thrilled about knocking back a few icy glasses, get me the ice bucket.

At what temperature do I serve red wines?
Room temperature is the standard rule. However, red wines provide ways for some serving temperature creativity. Who knew red wines could be chilled too? That was news to me in my early wine days.

Upon tasting certain reds chilled, they were surprisingly fantastic. Some reds that may be chilled are lighter in body, lower in tannin, and generally have a bright and lifted character overall. Grenache, Pinot Noir, and Gamay all fit these characteristics. A slight chill actually creates a fresher and livelier character in the wine.

So, unless you have this kind of wine, serve the wine at a normal room temperature. Some examples of room temperature wines are your everyday Cabernet Sauvignons, Malbecs, and Merlots, as well as any other medium- to full-bodied wine. Wines like this do well at room temperature because a chill would hide any nuances in the wine, much like white wines being served too cold. Also, the mouthfeel would be more astringent and sharper if you serve most red wine too cold.

One last temperature warning I must give you is to watch out that your wines don't get too warm. When wine sits in a hot car or has direct sunlight warming it up for too long, its character starts to change. If too warm, a wine starts oxidizing too rapidly and falls apart. The heat will start to change the makeup of the wine. The fruit will turn from fresh to baked, the wine will become flabby on the palate, and it will feel like the wine quite literally "cooked" on accident.

What is decanting, and do glasses make a difference for enjoying wine?

Decanting is another habitually misused word. The original understood meaning of this word was to take aged wine off the leftover sediment resulting from aging. This begs two questions: What is *sediment*? And what is *aging*?

There can be two pretty simple answers to these potentially rabbit-hole-type questions. Sediment in wine forms due to the flavor compounds, tannins, and color pigments breaking apart and falling out of suspension in the wine. The oxygen that slowly creeps through the microscopic holes in the cork cause this. Thus, *aging* is the slow evolution of a wine's color, aromas, and taste due to elongated periods of oxygen exposure.

Another usage of the word *decanting* has come to be associated with letting a wine "breathe." A lot of people only use the word *decanting* when referring to this activity. We know what the true meaning of the word indicates, but there is another accepted usage. One can use the word in this case to refer to trying to quickly loosen up a wine. When a wine truly ages, it naturally starts to unfurl and become even more complex and pleasing.

On the other hand, say you have a young, tight wine (Cabernet Sauvignon for instance) and it is a bit closed in and astringent. You want it to be slightly more loosened up and lush to drink in the moment. You can empty the wine into a vessel to rapidly expose it to oxygen and then let it sit for an hour or so. By doing this, you essentially achieve some of the changes age can bring, just in a more rapid fashion.

Another important aspect of serving wine is the glass you choose to serve it in. I used to be skeptical that the size or shape could really change how the wine smelled and tasted. David G. opened my eyes one day in the Inglenook bistro.

I kept accidently serving our high-end Cabernet Sauvignon "Rubicon" wine in the smaller all-purpose tasting glasses, instead of the larger-bowled Bordeaux glasses. Wanting to make sure I didn't make the mistake again, David poured the wine in both glasses and set them side by side. He told me to smell and taste both.

As I did, the all-purpose normal-sized glass gave the aromas and tastes I had expected. Then, when I explored the wine in the larger-bowled glass, my mind was blown. The aromas filled my nose more intensely. When I tasted the wine, it felt more mouth-filling and full of flavor. I was shocked and wondered what magic David had done.

The lesson here is that using specific glasses can enhance your wine-drinking experiences. I recommend investing in three different kinds of glasses. A Burgundy glass has a curved lip. A Bordeaux glass has a straight lip but a large bowl and opening at the top. A standard wine glass is medium sized with a standard lip and opening.

The magic of these glasses lies in how different your wine will taste in them. For instance, trying a Pinot Noir in the Burgundy glass will bring more of the subtle aromas to your nose. The glass will also guide the wine to hit the perfect spot on your palate. Drinking a Cabernet Sauvignon in a Bordeaux glass will help bring more oxygen to the wine, opening it up. Then, in the same way as the Burgundy glass, it will direct the wine to the perfect place on your palate for optimal enjoyment. The standard, or all-purpose, wine glass is perfect for a broader range of wines.

What is the proper way to store wine?
Wine storage doesn't have to be intimidating. The hardest part of the process is waiting years to drink a bottle you can't stop thinking about. With the following four tips, you can drastically reduce wine storage stress.

1. Age any and all wines out of sunlight.
2. Store wines somewhere with a temperature consistently between fifty-five and sixty-five degrees (don't constantly put wine through changes in temperature).

3. Lay the wine on its side. This ensures the wine has constant contact with the cork and will not oxidize too fast, but rather at a steadier pace.
4. Make sure the wine isn't moving around. You don't want to store the wine near anything that will rattle, vibrate, or cause physical motion to the wine. When a wine is moving and grooving the aging process is obstructed.

How do I know which wines age, and how long do I store them?
The part of wine aging many people don't realize is that only about 1 percent of the wines of the world are meant to age. That being said, you can imagine that wines capable of aging must have some pretty specific characteristics. The ability of some wines to blossom over time lies primarily in higher levels of sugar, acid, and tannin. All of these structural aspects help determine if a wine will succeed in aging. In addition, where the grapes are grown, the winemaking practices, and the initial aging practices of the winemaker influence the ability of a wine to stand the test of time.

Certain wines are made in such a way that the winemaker intends for them to be aged. Famous examples of wines that age very well are Cabernet Sauvignon from Bordeaux or Napa, Nebbiolo from Piedmont, Pinot Noir from Burgundy or Champagne, and Riesling from Mosel.

Another question I get constantly is, "How long do I age my wine?" I wish I could say that I could accurately tell you exactly how long to age every single wine you throw at me. I wish I knew the peak time to drink a wine at the drop of a hat. However, I can really only make a guess. I can gather clues about what grape variety the wine is made from, where it was made, and the producer to help me make an educated guess.

For instance, I would know a Nebbiolo from Piedmont has some of the highest tannins, acid, and intensity of flavor of all the wines in the world. Thus, a slow aging process would help soften the tannins, integrate the acid, and create more interesting aromas and flavors in the wine. For classic Piedmont producers and wines, I would know exactly what the quality of the wine is and how they intend for it to be aged. Conversely, I wouldn't know the exact intentions of a lesser-known winemaker and their distinctive vineyard sight. It's easy to generalize with wine, but because there so many exceptions, nuances, and individual producers out there, I devised a better way to reach the answers to your aging questions.

My end-all, be-all advice is to ask the people who made the wine in question. It's almost so simple you wonder why more people don't do it. For instance, you have a bottle of Sangiovese from Chianti. You were told you should age it, but have no idea for how long. The best thing to do is google the winery. Then either call or email them, asking for their suggestion for how long to age the wine. With this information, you'll know when your wine will hit its peak for you to enjoy it, and prevent the guessing game.

7

Fork in the Road

AFTER MY FIRST FEW WEEKS AT INGLENOOK, gaining Napa insights and living through my first earthquake, I started genuinely settling into the valley. On my days off, Katie and I would jump from winery to winery for tastings. Since we both worked in hospitality, all the tastings were complimentary. I discovered what I coined the "Napa buzz" during our first few tasting escapades. It's what happened after tasting at three or four wineries and feeling like everything was right in the world. Moreover, it embodied the afternoons of walking through vineyards and looking up at the sky, which had never seemed quite as blue before.

The glorious tastings proved I had a love affair with the sensations the valley could offer. However, frivolous wine tastings and actually studying wine were two entirely different things. I had the enjoyment of wine down pat, but was sorely lacking in any true vinous education.

It wasn't an enormous secret that I still knew next to nothing about wine; my first tasting surrounded by my peers had clearly proven that point. Day after day, I struggled to keep up with all the sommeliers and wine experts around me. Something kept telling me I needed to learn more. It was about time to turn the pleasure I found in wine into something more meaningful.

Every night after work I walked to my neighborhood Starbucks and read about wine. I stumbled through *The Wine Bible* by Karen McNeil, various Wine Folly online resources, and numerous *Wine Spectator* articles. They were the beginners' guides I desperately needed to start putting the puzzle pieces of wine together.

I returned home each night overwhelmed and full of espresso, but I didn't stop. I just kept going back night after night, finding new ways to study and build a foundation of knowledge. But I needed more than personal study sessions to keep my study fire going. I viewed Kyle, Matt, and David M. as the mighty three in the château. These men were the constant source of fuel for my fire to keep studying wine.

Kyle had the spirit and energy of a twentysomething boy trapped in a fortysomething's body. More importantly, he introduced himself as a sommelier. *Sommelier.* I had heard the word and vaguely knew what one did, but in reality, I had no clue. I never bothered asking so as not to put another nail in my clueless wine coffin.

Matt was a twentysomething guy, but with the decorum and presence of a forty-year-old. He was also a sommelier. While Kyle had something to say about every wine and shared his opinions at every moment, Matt was a bit more gracious and restrained with his wine knowledge.

Then there was David M. He was a slightly older gentleman, around sixty. He was not a sommelier but was certified through the Wine and Spirits Education Trust, and I always felt he had a more sentimental connection to wine.

As I envied these men and their knowledge, I struggled to grasp the different ways one could gain professional certification for wine. It turned out that the Court of Master Sommeliers, which Kyle and Matt were certified through, was specialized for restaurant sommeliers. The WSET program was geared more to academic minds and wine professionals not necessarily working in a restaurant setting. Both processes bewildered me, and I couldn't justify giving my time and energy to either. I resolved to continue my informal education.

Each day I silently listened to the knowledge swirling around me. I didn't dare speak up or add to the conversation when my expert peers were around, though I began feeling confident enough to share some of the wine facts I learned with guests of Inglenook. When I would surprise someone by telling them just one extra piece of information about the wine they were enjoying, or about grapevines, or about a piece of history with a certain grape, I felt immense fulfillment. It wasn't about knowing more than them; it was as if we were learning together.

A couple of months into my stay at Inglenook, a man named Pierre joined the team. He was quite a refreshing and unexpected addition to the cast of characters surrounding me. A Brazilian and a sommelier, he had a thick accent and a unique relationship with wine. Although he was way more advanced than I was, he had a similar drive to learn and share the elixir. We became fast friends. I maintained the belief that life put people in your path for a reason. He made studying wine feel accessible instead of over my head, like some of the others.

Pierre had an immense role in my growth with wine. He saw something in me I didn't quite even see myself. He could tell I had it in me to make something special of my desire to learn about wine. He never let me forget that. Every chance he had he would try to teach me a wine lesson—my own personal wine Yoda. He truly wanted to tutor me. I still wasn't sure what my next move would be in terms of a job, but I agreed to meet with him once a week to engage in structured wine studies. With my new guide, I felt myself beginning to make bigger strides with my studies.

For every action, there is an equal and opposite reaction. The opposite reaction to Pierre came in the form of a skeptical woman named Debbie, an older woman who ran the upstairs office at Inglenook. She worked somewhat in the background of the day-to-day activities of the château. I had met her my first day but didn't ever form much of a relationship with her.

Mind you, she was a matriarch of the Inglenook family. I simply didn't know her very well. It turned out she was interested in what I was trying to do there with my time in wine country. One particular morning, I was wiping down tables in the courtyard of the bistro when, surprisingly, Debbie engaged me with small talk about the weather and the view. We went back and forth for a few minutes.

The pleasantries ended, and she outright asked me what I was doing. I half wanted to answer I was wiping down tables, but the look in her eyes indicated that she meant with the direction of my life. I had mentally asked myself the same question daily. Hearing it asked out loud felt completely different. I couldn't help but flash back to my roommate's outburst and my own grandmother's reaction to my Napa decision. I tried not to miss a beat and told her I just wanted to learn about wine for a while. She looked at me as if I'd said something offensive. Her look told me I was delusional. She let me know I needed to get a real job and that it wasn't too late to do something with my life.

All my underlying fears rushed to the surface. Living the kind of life and taking the kind of chance with wine I had must've been the wrong choice. I had someone staring at me point-blank and telling me so.

I ended the conversation and calmed my fears with "We'll see what happens."

She seemed disinterested with that answer and said she hoped I would figure everything out. I went back behind the bistro counter, feeling small and avoiding letting people see my eyes moisten. As much as I didn't want to admit it, Debbie was right. I was a college graduate making coffees and pouring wines at a bistro. To me, it was a way into the world of wine I yearned for, but for the rest of the world, I must have looked lost.

As I continued to turn my eyes downward in the bistro, I remembered that my hopes rested on a forward gaze and movement. Action was the only way I had a chance to fight back doubts and fears. I needed something to use Debbie's words to take action in my own way. I decided then and there I was going to move up in the Inglenook world. I aspired to lead formal tastings and give wine tours of the property. All my wine idols in the château performed those jobs, and I affirmed I would be just like them.

I gave myself a timeline. I knew exactly when I needed to achieve the goal. My mom and dad had promised to visit me in October. I had it in my head that I would be able to show them my progress there doing formal tastings and tours by the time of their visit. My deadline marked my fourth month in the valley.

I doubled my studying efforts with Inglenook wines and read everything about the history of the property. Feeling ready, I went to my supervisor, David G., one day and told him I wanted to try my hand at formal tours and tastings. I came to find it was peculiar for bistro workers to want to move up so rapidly, but I was relentless. So David said we would work toward that role, and I would get my chance soon. I believed him, and, better yet, I believed in myself. I promised myself I would be out of my entry-level position and into a more respected role.

David was true to his word and let me do a bunch of shadowing with the true wine professionals of Inglenook. I followed along with more tours than I could count and tirelessly studied all the stories behind the wines we poured for our guests. I knew what made each one special and what the character of the grapes brought to the finished wine. I had done my homework and continued to do so. Every time I thought about giving in for the night or taking a break, I saw my grandmother and Debbie's doubtful eyes and vowed I would show them I could grow gracefully with wine and not just be a joke.

As many things do, my big break with Inglenook came suddenly and unexpectedly. It was a Sunday; David and I were in the bistro pouring a few glasses here and there, but nothing too dramatically busy. I loved afternoons when David and I had the chance to reflect on any number of topics.

The philosophizing didn't last long. In the early afternoon, Kyle came barreling down the caves from the Pennino (a formal tasting room at Inglenook) indicating they were completely in the weeds. All in all, there were only so many wine educators. There were just too many visitors and too few people to pour them wine. Kyle looked to David for help, and all he did was look at me.

"You're on, kid."

I didn't even hesitate. I threw off my black apron and followed a frantic Kyle down through the cellars to a room that had been off-limits to me until now. I caught Kyle's eyes rolling ever so slightly at the thought of me being able to actually help.

The Pennino was one of the most beautiful spaces I had seen in wine country. The stonework, the décor, and the stately nature of the room had captured my heart from the moment I stepped inside. I took one deep breath as I passed through the metal gates guarding its prestigious interior.

I saw David M. and Matt frantically trying to pour wines for a large number of guests and detail the subtle nuances of the stories and character behind each wine. They were struggling. Although I'm sure they doubted my abilities, they were glad to have some semblance of relief. I had been preparing, but I had never actually done a formal tasting for guests before. I looked to Kyle for guidance.

He said, "Take the wine, go to a table, pour a few ounces in each glass, and tell them about it."

Well, I presumed it really was that simple. I was nervous, but I grabbed my first white wine, called Blancenaux, and made my way to a table of two cozied in the corner. A million things flashed through my mind in that thirty-second walk with wine in hand. What if they knew more about wine than me? What if I messed up? What if I wasn't meant for this?

These questions had to take a backseat as I greeted them. They stared up at me with smiling faces, and I could tell they were just thrilled to be at this special place and tasting the lovely wines. My worries subsided, and I let loose.

I knew the wine, I loved the wine, and I shared all the information I found fascinating about it. They were engaged and intrigued. After my spiel, I turned away to return the bottle to the refrigerator and felt a rush of excitement. For the first time, my studies had paid off. The rest of the educators all gathered around to ask how it went. I told them I wanted to do it again, and they gave me table after table of visiting wine lovers.

We ended that Sunday afternoon all having a glass of wine to toast a job well done by all. I was most excited to have gained the respect of the people I had admired so greatly. I walked out of the château a little taller that evening. As I drove home with the sun setting over the mountains, I thought of how much joy I felt from sharing wine with people.

Every subsequent day when the Pennino guys would get in over their heads, I was called in. I pulled David G. aside one day and asked if I could wear a black or gray dress to work now because I might be in the formal tasting room and wanted to be ready. He agreed, and that was the end of my bistro uniform. This was at the end of September, and I charged in the direction of the goal I had set.

My parents would be in town in two weeks, and I wanted to guide them through a formal tasting. The tides had begun to change for me at Inglenook. I still wasn't a sommelier like them, but the wine guys began to treat me a bit differently. They started taking me ever so slightly more seriously. I continued my steadfast work to play both bistro hostess and wine educator at Inglenook. I can say those were some of the happiest times in my wine life. I knew enough about wine to get by, and I could appeal to both the novice and the seasoned wine veteran.

...

My parent's visit had arrived, and I had made my deadline. It was a Sunday, and my parents were due to fly into San Francisco that day. I happened to be in the bistro in my tasting-room dress that told the world I was more than just a café server. I was looking forward to meeting them for dinner. A group of people were gathered around the bistro counter that afternoon, and I was enthusiastically telling them all about the wine they were about to try. I glanced up and saw David G. at the entrance of the bistro with a huge smile across his face. Then I saw two of the most beautiful faces appear behind him. My mom and dad had surprised me.

I managed the last few pours for my group and made my way over to my parents with tears in my eyes. I couldn't help it. Seeing them for the first time in months and having worked so hard to make them proud overwhelmed me. I had never felt anything thing like it before. I seated them at one of the cozy bistro tables and poured them two hefty glasses of wine so they could enjoy the afternoon sipping Napa Cab and watching me do a job I truly loved.

I spent a week wining and dining them in the valley I had come to hold so dear to my heart. I fulfilled my dream of hosting them in the Pennino room as a blossoming wine professional. I felt amazing about how far I had come and that I was able to make their trip memorable. Unlike my grandmother or Debbie, they never demanded more of me and knew I was happy being able to grow with wine. They knew I was striving to make it in that valley, and they were thrilled for me. They left, and I promised to only keep getting better.

I continued my simultaneous work in the bistro and Pennino. One day, I was hosting a very friendly young couple. After the wine talk was done, we dove into some small talk. They asked the question that seemed to be on every visitor's mind: How did I come to work with wine in Napa Valley? I told them my abbreviated version of how I found myself standing in front of them, and they were intrigued by every word. Feeling comfortable with them, I inquired as to what they did for work. The man said he worked for Disney, and my ears automatically perked up.

Disney was the company I would have given anything to work for straight out of college if it hadn't been for my move toward wine. Disney could have given me stability and a position at a well-respected company. I obviously wanted to learn more about what he did. We continued talking, and I learned he didn't just work for Disney, but he was very high up in the chain of command within the organization. Almost surprised at the words out of my mouth, I shared with him that I might be looking for a way to use my college degree after I finished my "wine adventure."

I told him how much the thought of working for the Disney Corporation meant to me. As I kept their glasses full, we shared more and more conversation. The afternoon ended with him giving me his business card and telling me to reach out about job opportunities. His name was Mark. He possibly held the key to opening the door to a "real" job for me. I loved wine, but a glimmering promise of a legitimate career still caught my eye. I had a chance to work with a respected company using my college degree. I knew I had to at least pursue possible options.

I emailed him the very next day about wanting to move forward with trying to work for Disney. We exchanged a few emails, and with every response from him, I felt myself betraying wine. It didn't feel right, but for some reason, it felt necessary. It was as though I couldn't keep the wine fairy tale up any longer. I came to the conclusion that working for Disney would never make me as happy as wine, but I figured that was what growing up meant. Mark put me in contact with a head recruiter working at the main offices in Burbank. Her name was Marsha, and our correspondence ensued.

I sent her my résumé, and she let me know she would be thrilled to meet with me. With a potential meeting waiting for me, I knew I had to make some serious moves. I told her I would be in LA the following week and would love to meet with her. I lied and planned a trip just for one woman who could possibly put me on a fast track toward a more conventional job and life.

True to form, I just went for it. I packed an overnight bag and drove off for LA from Napa. I didn't even tell anyone. I almost wanted to turn back up in town with a brand-new, prestigious job and surprise everyone. I drove eight hours down through the heart of California and stayed in a hostel in West Hollywood. The unglamorous nature of the hostel should have come as no surprise to me. I crawled into my bottom bunk bed in the hostel and tried to get some sleep before the potentially life-changing meeting with Marsha the next morning.

I woke up early the next morning determined to squeeze as much out of the trip as possible. I took in some of Hollywood, and it was an experience, but I felt out of place for some reason. I couldn't shake the seemingly pretentious nature of it all. After a couple of hours roaming the staple sites—Rodeo Drive, the Hollywood sign, the Walk of Fame—I made my way to the Disney Studios in Burbank.

I walked into my meeting with a mixture of excitement and uncertainty. I had my résumé and a professional outfit, and I reverted to the career-searching mindset I had back at UF. I prepared to say all the right things and had practiced my interviewing skills countless times with my pursuit of advertising jobs in the past.

I was greeted by a middle-aged woman with kind eyes. Her office was distinguished yet decked out with classic Disney charm. She introduced herself as Marsha and ushered me in to have a seat. We chatted about how I had come to meet her boss, Mark, and how I was enjoying my visit to LA. The formalities ended, and we dove into my interest in a position with Disney.

We went over my résumé and school experience and what exactly I would want to do in terms of work with the company. I recited everything I was supposed to and stated I would be interested in working in the marketing arena. We went over what strengths I could bring to the table and what weaknesses I possessed.

Then she asked the question I had been waiting for. How the heck did an advertising major from the University of Florida find herself all the way out in Napa Valley working at a winery? I had wanted to stay off the topic of wine, as I figured it would do very little to help me land a marketing job with them. Since she had expressed such a strong interest, I discussed my journey, wine study, and working at Inglenook. My demeanor grew relaxed, and it wasn't a job interview anymore and felt as though I was talking to a friend.

She inquired more about what exactly I did with wine, and I could tell it was fascinating to her. I couldn't help it—I jabbered on about wine, what I was learning about it, and the magic of Napa. Her eyes only grew larger and larger.

Her final question in the interview was, "Do you love what you are doing now?"

I knew I should've told her yes, but not as a career. I should've gone into how I wanted to move into a more professional position and use my college degree. But those weren't the words that left my lips. Her point-blank question made me realize working with wine had a hold on my heart.

I answered her by saying I loved it and that I woke up excited to go to work every morning. A deep smile spread across her face, and she asked me why I would do anything else. I told her I didn't know if it could be a career for me. She expressed something to me that has stayed with me to this day. She told me that when I talked about wine I lit up. My energy and enthusiasm for what I was doing were palpable. She said I had found my passion and it would be a shame to lose it.

The interview had taken a very unexpected turn. She turned into my own personal fairy godmother. She assured me that some people never have a chance to work with something they love. Her genuine advice stirred something inside me. I left the interview without a job with Disney, but with the resolution I would become a certified sommelier. I left with the confidence I could be a sommelier and make a career out of wine.

From that day on, I would never let anyone make me feel small for choosing a life of wine. I had come to a great crossroads, and I chose my path. I would forever be grateful to her for refusing to let me pursue a career that threatened to take even the smallest bit of light from my eyes.

A week later, I sent her a bottle of wine and a note expressing thanks for her encouragement. I promised I would become a sommelier. I told her that because of her, I would never give up my passion. It was the first time I expressed becoming a sommelier as a goal. Writing it down made it real. It would be up to me to make it come true.

From the moment I arrived back in Napa from LA, I knew what I truly wanted to do with wine. I enrolled in all the necessary courses and dug in. If I was going to do this, I was going to throw everything I had at the goal. I was bound and determined to study through the Court of Master Sommeliers and the Wine and Spirit Education Trust at the same time. These organizations are the leaders in certifying wine professionals. They both require students to have a deep knowledge of wine production, regions, styles, tasting, and everything in between.

In addition to the theory side, there was another aspect that was challenging and intimidating to me: I had to learn how to blind taste wine. Unless I could master the skill of blind tasting, I would never pass any level of WSET or become a certified sommelier through the CMS. Both organizations required proficiency in tasting wine blind in tandem with deep wine theory knowledge.

Lucky for me it seemed, the sommeliers of Inglenook had a tasting group that met in the château in the early morning once a week. I had always watched and listened to them go back and forth discussing many different wines. The thought of trying to guess a wine's identity blind seemed nearly impossible to me, but after my LA experience, I knew what I had to do. I had to get myself in their group no matter how much of a hopeless taster I was. The wine education path I resolved to follow was undoubtedly uphill, but nothing could stop my climb.

Wine Talk: Tannins, Hangovers, and Sulfites

Bachelorette parties in Napa were my first crash course in attempting to understand what tannins and sulfites actually were in relation to hangovers. Inglenook was a popular destination for gaggles of ladies ready to "let loose" in wine country. Without fail, one or two of the ladies would say they were allergic to tannins or sulfites or that red wines gave them more of a hangover. They would ask me why red wines would do that to them, and I avoided the question I didn't know the answer to by distracting them with copious bottles of sparkling wine.

The constant questions regarding the correlation between those elements in wine and hangovers made me dive deeper into the subject. After doing some digging, I discovered a few flaws to the claims. Overall, less than 1 percent of our population is allergic to tannins. Also, there are far more sulfites in dried fruits than in any bottle of wine. Most importantly, neither one can be linked to a greater hangover the next day.

Having the right idea of what tannins and sulfites truly are will help you ask wine professionals more informed questions about the wines they serve you. Even better, you'll better understand your potential reactions to wine and how to avoid the dreaded hangover.

How will it feel to sip a wine with low or high alcohol?

You may be starting to gather that when you take a sip of wine there is *a lot* going on. If you have a basic understanding of the main components, it can be all the more fun to drink. Alcohol certainly plays a role in the overall merriment of wine. Our friend alcohol comes about when yeast eats up the sugar in grape juice; that's the gist of fermentation. And the two byproducts are alcohol and carbon dioxide.

Alcohol can be high, low, or medium in wines. High-alcohol wines will have a certain warmth down the back of the palate. You will actually feel a heat. That's why wine people will sometimes call a wine "hot" if it has noticeably high alcohol. High alcohol can also be associated with a certain glycerol (richer) taste.

Lower-alcohol wines will have the exact opposite effect. They won't have that heat and sweet feel. Medium-alcohol wines, as you can imagine, fall somewhere in the middle. Some wine people feel that with less alcohol you get to experience more of the true character of the grape. High alcohol can actually be used to mask low-quality wines.

We now know what alcohol feels like, but the more interesting part is what causes wines to have more or less of it. Climate, the level of ripeness of grapes at harvest, and winemaker decisions impact alcohol levels. Warmer climates typically point to a higher alcohol level, while cooler climates typically produce less. This is because in warm climates the grapes have the potential to acquire more sugar, and more sugar in the juice during fermentation means the yeast can eat up more sugar and produce greater amounts of alcohol.

In addition to natural conditions, winemakers can use certain techniques to influence alcohol levels. Say we are in chilly Mosel, Germany. The Riesling grapes struggle to ripen fully and have a noticeably low level of sugar at harvest. In order to increase the alcohol potential, winemakers use a technique called *chaptilization*. This means they add sugar to the grape juice prior to fermentation. This technique is what allows Mosel Rieslings to have adequate alcohol levels, because the yeast has more sugar to turn into alcohol.

Say we go to the other end of the spectrum; we are in Barossa Valley in Australia. The Shiraz (Syrah) grapes acquire high amounts of sugar before harvest because of the heat. The juice is full of sugar, and the resulting wine will have a higher than acceptable alcohol percentage. The winemaker can use what's called *reverse osmosis* to reduce the amount of alcohol in the wine.

Simply put, reverse osmosis is the technique of putting a wine through microscopic filtration and distillation to separate the alcohol from the water in the wine. A portion of alcohol is distilled out, while the water and all the other elements of wine remain. The *distillation of alcohol* is another way of saying it's evaporated out and the overall alcohol level is lowered.

What is the purpose of sulfites?
Sulfites sound scary and can perhaps deter one from enjoying a glass.

The real purpose of sulfites is as a preservative and to promote a "cleaner" wine. Sulfites merely stabilize and create a more polished finished product. The addition of sulfites acts as a preventative measure against unwanted oxidation and microbial activity in the wine. Some hardcore wine producers completely avoid the usage of sulfites, and this simply leads to a more rustic and natural feel in the finished wine.

Are sulfites bad? Do natural wines have no sulfites?
The fact that the bottle warns us of the presence of sulfites doesn't mean we have to run screaming from wine. In general, sulfites are preservatives and antioxidants. The baseline misunderstanding of them is what causes a general concern. Sulfites are found in very minuscule proportions in wine and occur naturally anyway. Sulfites are really only dangerous to people with serious asthmatic conditions (about 1 percent of the total population).

Sulfites can cause alarm when they are used liberally during various points of the winemaking process. Less health-conscious winemakers use high levels of sulfur to grow grapes, make wine, and mask imperfections in finished wines. In these cases, it's worth thinking about substituting other options for those wines.

An option that exhibits a low- to no-sulfur approach is natural wines. Natural wines aim to avoid man's addition of sulfites. The point of natural wines is to have the most hands-off approach possible. On the whole, natural wines will seem slightly less polished and truly exhibit the character of the individual grape being used. Sulfites are still produced as a natural byproduct of fermentation. The key to natural wines is that sulfur is not added to try to make grapes, wine, or any finished products something that they're not.

So, sulfur and sulfites in wine have the potential to be harmful if there is an attitude of overusage and a lack of concern for purity in the wine.

What do tannins feel like?

Tannins can be confusing. Remember, tannins are the phenolic compounds found in the skin of grapes, oak barrels, and the seeds of grapes. Even if you conceptually know what they are and where they come from, it can be unclear what they actually feel like.

Here are the best ways to try to pinpoint tannins in your sip of wine. Imagine you steeped tea for too long and took a sip. That bitter, astringent liquid sensation is the same sensation tannin in wine can bring you.

Another example would be biting into apple skin. The drying, bitter taste of apple skin is another way to imagine what you are looking for with tannins. Using the apple example helps lock in the fact that tannins help balance out a wine. Much like how apple skin brings texture to a bite of apple, tannins bring texture to wine.

So the next time you sip wine run your tongue along your gums and the roof of your mouth. By doing this, you can more clearly feel for the griping, bitter sensation of tannin. The more dried out and rough your tongue feels, the higher the tannin level in the wine. Lower-tannin wines, in theory, will be easier to drink and not dry you out as much. Thus, lower-tannin wines can be perceived as easier to drink.

The way a winemaker manages tannins is something to consider as well. Tannin brings texture and grip to your palate, but a winemaker can influence the way tannin is perceived. Let's look at a grape varietal with high levels of tannin and how two different winemakers might work with it.

Cabernet Sauvignon genetically has high tannins. A winemaker can reduce the impact and drying nature of the high tannins by letting the grape ripen longer. A longer ripening will cause the tannins in the skin of the grape to become less intense. Also, the grapes will have more sugar upon harvest. The higher sugar will lead to a wine with more alcohol and body. The structure of the wine will also distract from the tannins of the wine.

On the opposite end of the spectrum, say a winemaker wants to make a Cabernet Sauvignon showing astringent, grippy, and noticeable tannin. An earlier grape picking time is one way to ensure more under-ripe, or "green," tannins in a finished wine. Also, there will be less sugar in the grapes at harvest. This results in less alcohol and body, which can make the tannins even easier to perceive.

Finally, fermenting the juice of red grapes with the actual stems of the grapes can add more tannins to the finished wine. Instead of destemming the grapes prefermentation, the winemaker simply crushes whole clusters and throws everything into a fermentation vessel. The stems add even more phenolic bitterness, or tannin, to the wine. This technique is called *whole-cluster fermentation*.

Do full-bodied red wines with lots of tannins give me a worse hangover?

Trust me, I hate a hangover as much as the next person. The most important point I can get across is that higher-tannin wines don't lead to stronger hangovers. The myth that red wines cause worse hangovers just isn't true. As you now know, tannins are the phenolic compounds that create bitterness in wine. Tannins don't have any correlation to alcohol. The alcohol in wine is what causes dehydration, which in turn causes a hangover the morning after a wine-drinking marathon.

There's no scientific proof that tannin polymers have an effect on hangovers. Also, red wines don't necessarily point to a more intense hangover either. The only minor difference when thinking about a hangover is that whites have lower alcohol levels on the whole. That being said, more alcohol can impact your health the next day. Hangovers are truly the result of dehydration and lack of food consumption during drinking.

8

So You Want to Be a Sommelier?

SOMETHING IN ME CHANGED after my meeting with Marsha. Nothing could stop me from making my dream of becoming a sommelier come true. However, my head wasn't entirely up in the clouds. I had seen the documentary *Somm* on Netflix, and it struck me with the realization I was in for a challenge the likes of which I had never seen before.

The film followed three potential master sommelier candidates through their quests to pass the daunting master exam. It captured all the moments of struggle as they prepared to pass the rigorous test. As I watched them drilling notecards, tasting wines, and going through tedious wine service, the reality of my difficult task hit me. My actual test to become a certified sommelier would be considerably less challenging, but at the time, everything seemed vastly more intimidating than I had imagined before watching the documentary.

Despite whether I could achieve the title of sommelier or not, my decision to pursue it had a deep meaning for me. I was going down a path that looked absolutely crazy but felt so incredibly right. I hadn't thought about how it looked to the outside world. I was drifting further and further away from normalcy. As I told friends and family that my time in Napa wasn't just temporary anymore, I was met with mixed reviews. Many friends thought it was cool, but the majority of people were just confused as to why I would do this. I learned something—my dream only had to make sense to me.

As I began to fully commit to my life's new direction, I let the wine-savvy gentlemen I worked with know my plans. Kyle and David M. were concerned about my aggressive push to try to become both WSET Level 3 certified and a certified sommelier within one year. My coworkers did a good job of making me feel the weight of the goal I had chosen to pursue. They were also a mix of supportive and doubtful bystanders. Many offered luck, but their eyes told me they didn't truly believe I could do it. They had witnessed all my novice wine occasions and knew how much I needed to improve. They believed I was young and inexperienced, compared to essentially any other aspiring sommelier.

The only way I knew how to get it done was to give myself a nearly impossible deadline. I decided I had to put my head down and grind it out. My wine quest was going to be a test of skills I'd never dreamed of having. Opposed to every other test I had ever taken, I actually wanted to take this one.

As I crafted my study plan, I decided to work toward my WSET Level 3 Award and my Court of Master Sommeliers certification at the same time. I resolved to skip levels 1 and 2 of the WSET and go straight for level 3, due to the confidence I gained from my nightly Starbucks study trips. As I plunged into the books for WSET level 3, I realized my confidence was unwarranted, but I had gotten myself into the wine whirlwind, so, regardless, I had to succeed no matter what. WSET presented an attainable achievement through unrelenting studious review, but the real challenge in my eyes was to become a certified sommelier.

I went on the court's website to view the limited number of testing dates offered for certification. The only date that would work was in October, seven months away. One part of me shouted this was too soon, and I would never make it. The other part screamed to reach out and grab the opportunity with every ounce of strength I had. I threw caution to the wind and signed up for the exam, which would mark my six-month anniversary in Napa.

If I could pull it off, I would have gone from zero to sommelier in less than a year and a half. I decided to keep it as my secret. I needed the goal to be mine and mine alone. I had no desire to hear words of caution that would keep me from pursuing my goal. My plan may have been crazy, but I didn't need anyone to tell me to my face just how impossible it was.

Pierre was, by far, my staunchest advocate. He wanted me to show everyone at Inglenook I had what it took to be a sommelier. Something in his voice told me I had a special gift for wine. Pierre set up a study plan to help me keep growing. He didn't quite know my outlandish plan to become a sommelier, but recognized how much I needed to learn. I felt as though he saw a bit of himself in my passion and intrigue for wine. He assured me we would meet early one morning a week to check on my progress and blind taste.

Now, blind tasting was more intimidating to me than any other wine challenge. To make matters worse, all the guys I worked with and other wine professionals from around Napa would meet to blind taste at Inglenook one morning a week. They would take up a full table in one of our tasting caves. Ten to twelve distinguished-looking winos would sit in front of rows of glasses. They would gaze at, smell, sip, and then spit out the wine. I generally stared at them, entranced as each person would share their thoughts on the wine. Then they would guess what was in their glasses.

In the beginning, I viewed it as some kind of supernatural power. Oh, how badly I wanted to achieve the power to do what they did. I envisioned myself peering into the soul of a wine and having it gently whisper its identity. There were only two problems with my aspirations: I wasn't even invited to the table, and I still had no clue how to begin to search for anything in a wine.

Upon further research, I resolved blind tasting was all about connecting the cognitive to the sensory. I could have had the best nose and palate in the world, but I needed the knowledge to connect everything together. I figured out I would need to put in the work no one enjoyed. I would read every book I could get my hands on, I would drill grape profiles, I would draw maps of every major wine region, and I would dive into a subject I had only scratched the surface of.

I started seeing myself surpass the less advanced wine professionals at work. I still couldn't hold a candle to the likes of Kyle, David M., Pierre, and Matt, but I wasn't a deer in the headlights anymore. As my confidence grew, I felt it was time I asked the blind-tasting gatekeepers to let me sit in with them. I longed to be in their mystical tasting room. I asked Kyle and David M. one morning if I could merely sit and watch them. My request was met with intense opposition.

I accepted the rejection. It was hard to fight hard for something that scared me in the first place. It would take someone to do the fighting for me. Pierre wouldn't let up on them to let me join the tasting group. He regularly tasted with the group and promised me he would get me in.

Pierre must have done a good bit of persuading because he approached me the next day and told me I could sit in the following week. As he was telling me, I saw Kyle out of the corner of my eye shake his head and smile.

Leading up to my first tasting group session, I crammed information about every major grape I could find. I realized I hadn't tasted half of them. I also learned there was something called a "grid" that sommeliers used to try to analyze the wines in front of them. The grid contained twenty-five different categories of what to look for in the wine. My major challenge was to figure out what all the categories actually meant. I needed to know what to look for.

My first day with the group arrived. We all met at 7:30 a.m. in a tasting room. The thought of even putting wine in my mouth at that hour was unsettling, even if I would be spitting it out. I went through the grand front doors that morning with a sense of being in the "cool kids" club. I made it into a tasting group. One more step closer to becoming a sommelier.

I passed through the caves to the tasting room. Reaching the door, I observed the discerning and knowledgeable faces of the other members; then I took a deep breath and turned the handle. To my surprise, a spot was set up for me in front of a full set of glasses. I was both terrified and thrilled as the glasses of wine just stared back at me.

As I stared at the wines wishing I knew what they were, a gentleman in the group broke the silence and confidently said he would analyze the first wine. His name was Andrew. He was a larger biker-type dude. Regardless of what he looked like, he poetically fit every box of the grid to this particular wine. He described it perfectly and recited the vintage of the wine, the grape, and the exact region it was from. I thought, *There is no way this biker dude nailed the wine.*

The group leader revealed it. The wine was a 2014 Sauvignon Blanc from Sancerre in France. Andrew didn't miss a single thing. I would have been doing a victory dance, but he simply smiled and nodded his head. Would the day ever come when I could do what he did? That's all I could think about the rest of the day. I was determined to possess those skills. There wasn't going to be a glamorous way to get to his level. I would have to return week after week and taste new wine after new wine.

Another week had passed with my new 7:30 a.m. wine tradition. I was still content to sit on the sidelines and simply listen to the wine banter, but Pierre said they should let me take a shot at one of the wines. I thought they would brush off the suggestion and collectively agree I needed more time to develop the skills. To my shock, it was my turn at bat, and with each nodding head, I felt my eyes grow wider and my heart rate speed up. I would have to plunge into the wine at some point and just see where the chips fell.

I grabbed the glass, gave it a few twirls, and began my first attempt. To say I stumbled through the wine would be generous. I forgot most of the grid, and of the parts I did remember, I was off by a mile when describing the wine in my hand. It couldn't have gone much worse, but I finally reached the part of the analysis where I was required to guess a grape. I completely froze. I shifted through grape profiles in my head for what felt like twenty minutes, until someone asked if I wanted to call a grape. My mind was completely blank. I said the first grape I could think of, California Chardonnay, probably because that was the first wine I tasted with my parents. I was praying the wine gods would give me a gift. I took a shot in the dark and thought maybe by a miracle I would nail the wine.

I still had a shred of hope, until someone at the head of the table burst out laughing, subsequently making me think, *Thanks a lot, wine gods*. I looked up and saw Kyle uproariously laughing at my guess. I looked around and saw faces of people with a mix of pity and humor staring back at me. I don't remember what the wine was, but I remember what the day made me feel. I felt like a worthless joke.

I wore a fake smile the rest of the tasting and tried to laugh off my horrible performance. As I drove away from Inglenook that morning, I felt wet tears streaming down my face. I was at my lowest and most doubtful point. Part of me wanted to keep crying and drive all the way back to Florida. I questioned if I belonged in the world of wine at all.

About ten minutes into my drive, the sun was beginning to peek over the mountains and illuminating the vines as I drove past. For the moment, I forgot my feelings of failure, embarrassment, and dejection. The scene in front of me reminded me that I still loved the study of wine, and no one could steal that from me. A small voice inside me told me I had to go back next week. I wiped away my tears and vowed to myself I would show them what I was capable of.

I went back the next week with an unshakable will. Many of them assumed I wouldn't dare show my face again. I took a blind wine again and had the same stumbling failure. No one laughed this week, and I saw it as a step in the right direction.

After the tasting, I discovered that Andrew would be joining the Inglenook wine team. I found this announcement slightly odd because the man had come from the likes of The French Laundry. The French Laundry is by far one the most famous restaurants in all the world, thus making it the icon of dining in Napa. The wine list and team were considered the best in California. He had been working there as a sommelier but decided to work with us. I was confused, but I assumed the pressure of a restaurant could wear a person down. Regardless of my questions concerning his job shift, I knew his presence would add a whole new dimension to my beloved Inglenook.

After the tasting that morning, we had a chance to talk. I welcomed him to Inglenook, and I could already tell he had an air of superiority. I paid no real attention to it, hoping he was just nervous about the new position. He went into the fact that he was going for his advanced certification with the Court and working with Inglenook to allow himself more time to study. It all made sense now. He saw this as the cushy job he needed to prepare to become an advanced sommelier. It didn't take long for me to realize how Andrew would change my day-to-day life. His coming on with us meant every wine professional at Inglenook was a certified sommelier or at least WSET certified.

The wine banter between us all intensified. He and Kyle had an especially friendly competition about who could spout off more wine facts. I did love it when he could shut Kyle down. He was the kind of person who made you rise to the occasion—someone who had the ability to make you dig a bit deeper however uncomfortable it was at the moment. Everything was a wine question, challenge, or discussion.

I wasn't in Kansas anymore. Andrew was the real thing. He stood for all the somms I had ever seen in documentaries or on TV. Although most times he made me feel like a complete idiot, I knew he had the ability to push me, if he knew it or not.

He approached me one day and said he had heard I was going to try to become a certified sommelier. I told him I absolutely wanted to become certified. He had a subtle smirk on his face and asked if I knew just what I was undertaking. I let the direct question sink in a moment. I thought I knew what was required of me from tips Kyle and Matt had told me and general banter around my wine friends throughout Napa. But the way he was looking at me told me I didn't have the first real clue. He fired off three questions about wine styles, producers, and geography. My mind was completely blank. He told me if I didn't know those, I had a long way to go.

The rapid-fire questioning wiped the smile off my face, but he wasn't done yet. He asked me if I knew what I was in for with the service portion of the certified exam. I slightly nodded my head. He asked me how many times I had practiced mock service, and I could only shake my head to indicate I hadn't. He proceeded to let me know I would need to pour right-handed (as a left-hander I didn't think that was a requirement); know copious food-and-wine pairings to answer on the spot; know all the major producers of the world and every major cocktail and dessert wine, aperitif, and digestive; and be prepared to answer questions about all these things while properly opening a bottle of sparkling wine in front of a master sommelier.

I knew bits and pieces of all this, but never had my passing the certified exam seemed so far out of reach than standing in front of Andrew that day. With my head still spinning, I thanked him for the reality check and turned away. If his goal was to intimidate the hell out of me, he succeeded with flying colors. As I walked toward my car to head home, I felt the same familiar hopelessness of the blind-tasting scenario. I wouldn't let myself cry this time. I didn't have time to doubt myself and feel small anymore. I had a test to pass.

I pulled away from Inglenook and headed into town. I went directly to the supermarket and bought a case of sparkling wine, four flute glasses, and cupcakes. I texted Katie, who was living with me at that point, and asked if she felt like sparkling wine and cupcakes that night. My plan was to practice service in front of her until I was sick of it. Then I would go before Andrew and see how I stacked up. In my heart, I knew there was no turning back.

Wine Talk: Study Tips

The most poignant point I can make is it doesn't matter where you begin when you study wine. The most helpful thing you can do for yourself is to simply begin. I was fortunate to have fate nudge me in that direction. Perhaps fate could be trying to push you as well. Much like many points of my wine journey, the study of wine seemed like an insurmountable mountain of information to climb. Just remember the key to learning more and sticking with it is to keep moving forward.

My most useful lessons were the times when I was dead wrong. I have felt the necessary and uncomfortable sensation of not knowing a *thing*. My public Zinfandel mix-up at Inglenook certainly proved that necessity. However, being able to share the knowledge you achieve makes it all worth it. So don't be afraid to begin, take the missteps in stride, and savor the moments of wine expertise when you achieve them.

How does one study wine?

A fantastic part of wine is why and how you choose to learn more about it. You can be the everyday drinker wanting to uncover wine's mystery, you can be the collector wanting to have greater insights into your prized bottles, you can aspire to make wine your professional vocation, or anything in between. Learning about wine can be as relaxed or in-depth as you make it. I guarantee, whether you scratch the surface or take a deep dive like I did, you will find joy in it.

Since I took the plunge with wine and became a sommelier, people have constantly asked how I became one and if it was hard. Anything worth working toward should be hard, and yes, sommelier certification is no exception. To begin really learning about wine you have to do far more than just drink copious amounts of wine. For me, it all started with books. Getting familiar with wine terminology and all the basics was the only place to start in my mind.

The other big part is not to get overwhelmed. The world of wine is vast and intimidating, but taking small steps every day to expand your knowledge makes wine vastly more interesting and fun. Also, putting the simple concepts you learn into practice can help lock them in your mind. So if you are reading about Tuscan wine, have a classic Italian meal with a Chianti. Of course, share the experience with someone else and tell them everything you know about the wine.

Simply put, the best answer as to how to study is to start. Go out and buy a classic book about wine today. Reading about wine more extensively will help your mind to start learning the language. Once you speak the language of wine, learning becomes much more fluid (excuse the pun).

Should I take formal wine classes?

Formal classes were a necessity for me to attain the certifications to make this my profession. The WSET provided an online resource to help me find classes in my area. Also, the CMS offered classes throughout the country you could find online. Essentially, Google, social media, and engaging with local wine professionals will be your best bets to tracking classes down.

For someone more interested in wine as a hobby, formal classes may not give you what you want. If you want the study of wine to be an engaging hobby, I recommend you learn about it in the most engaging ways possible. Try creating a wine club with others who want to learn. Have monthly meetups focusing on a particular wine and region, and do some self-study. You can all get together to discuss what you learned about the topic and taste wines relating to it—educational and delicious!

Also, visiting wine regions around the world can be very educational if you truly go to try to learn. In addition, listening during tastings a bit closer, taking time to research some of the wines you taste, and actively discussing wine with friends can lead to a greater understanding.

How do you become a certified sommelier?

Say you want to make wine more than a hobby. You want to make a career out of learning about and sharing this glorious drink. You resolve to become a certified sommelier. Now, how to go about doing it.

The formal body that provides the testing and certification of wine professionals is the Court of Master Sommeliers. The three main cornerstones of becoming a professional sommelier are book knowledge, blind tasting, and wine service. These three categories must be mastered and constantly kept sharp. Aside from knowing what you are getting into, I recommend going on CMS' website and signing up for the introductory course. It is taught by master sommeliers and has a multiple-choice exam at the end. If this exam is passed, you will be qualified to continue testing for the certified level.

After this, things become more serious. The certified exam will require much more focused study of the three facets of wine I outlined earlier. Aside from my advice, having a mentor is essential to wine study. Find a certified sommelier and let them know your wine aspirations, and I can guarantee they will want to help by even just offering some words of advice.

What is the WSET?

The dynamic nature of wine allows you to attack it from a lot of different angles. I saw this firsthand from my Inglenook wine experts. Kyle and Matt had been certified through the Court of Master Sommeliers. The WSET, which stands for the Wine and Spirit Education Trust, operates out of England and is an entirely different organization to go through when formally studying wine. An interesting way to distinguish between the Court of Master Sommeliers and the WSET is in what the material is geared toward. Yes, wine is wine, but there can be different ways to approach it.

WSET is more scholastic and provides an in-depth "book smart" kind of feel. The Court of Master Sommeliers is more of the "street smart" feel. This just means the WSET gives you more structured study material geared to a scholastic understanding of wine. The Court of Master Sommeliers offers much less formal study material and instead recommends more literature for you to explore on your own.

The Court of Master Sommeliers' main objective is to prepare its students for more restaurant work as a sommelier. They emphasize the knowledge of producers, wine pairings, and the art of serving wine.

Whichever organization you go through, you will have a greater grasp on wine through their program.

What are the best books to read for wine education?

I asked many of my coworkers at Inglenook where to start with my studying. I received a myriad of different answers, but Matt (a young sommelier at Inglenook) gave me the recommendation I stuck with. He told me to read *Wine for Dummies*. He assured me he wasn't being obnoxious, but rather the book really provided a useful overview of wine. The book assumes you know next to nothing about wine and opens the door to better wine understanding. He told me if I could get through it and enjoy reading it, that would be a good sign that studying wine would be for me. After reading it, I wanted more. If you are the same, then you will dig deeper as well.

Other books that were enormously helpful for me when I was starting out were *The Wine Bible* by Karen Macneil, *Windows on the World: The Complete Wine Course* by Kevin Zraly, and *How to Taste: A Guide to Enjoying Wine* by Jancis Robinson. These were my go-tos because they straddled the line between precise and readable. They all offered facts and figures without being too dry. The authors felt like wine's storytellers. They made wine knowledge feel attainable, rather than intimidating.

9

Chorizo and Clams

SEVEN MONTHS WENT by faster than I ever imagined possible. Not a day went by without me studying, tasting, or serving wine. It was late October, and my exam was a week away. I was chomping at the bit to see if I had grown in the knowledge and service of wine I longed for. I had essentially cleaned out my local grocery store of every cheap bottle of sparkling wine they had. I turned my cozy breakfast nook into a mock restaurant. Night after night, I practiced my service presentation. Katie and Mater, her golden retriever, would sit down for fake dinner and ask me various wine questions. I was slowly getting better at opening and pouring sparkling wine, answering tough pairing questions, knowing all the classic cocktails in the world, and the tedious steps of sparkling wine service. It appeared my loyal friend and her dog would be just the support I needed to achieve the seemingly unattainable goal.

The time had come: I asked Andrew to critique my service. I knew the exam was exactly five days away, but he had no clue. I wanted to keep it that way. I had a shred of hope I could actually pass the test. I set everything up in the tasting room at Inglenook, and he sat at my mock restaurant table. I took a deep breath and began the steps of service. There was something different about my movements, thought processes, and overall comfort. I was nervous because I knew his feedback would be honest and harsh. His words had power over me. I made service mistakes, and my bottle made a huge popping sound, contrary to what was required by the court. I stumbled and stuttered with my answers entirely too much. I knew I was better than this performance. My performance in front of Andrew wasn't what I had worked for all those months.

As I finished, I already knew his review of my work would be less than glowing. I looked at him and hoped maybe he would say I had done better than I thought. Instead, he told me a million and one things I had missed or done incorrectly and what needed massive improvement. My heart fell into my stomach. He wished me better luck next time. He said not to worry, though; maybe in a year or so I could be ready to take the exam.

As I cleaned up, my mind raced and doubt started creeping in. The same feeling of inadequacy I'd battled at the beginning of studying tried to take over. I didn't let it in, but rather I let it drive me to fine-tune my skills. I was short on time, but I was going to master everything I slipped up with during my last service before my exam. I certainly wasn't about to give up at the last mile of this race I was running.

The last four days before my test, my mind was only seeing soil types, grape varieties, vinification techniques, and iconic producers. I must have fallen asleep envisioning my steps of service every night leading up to D-day. I was taking a day off of work in order to drive to San Francisco and sit for the exam at the Sir Francis Drake Hotel. The morning I was set to head off to the city, I had my final tasting at Inglenook. The wines we focused on were Pinot Grigio and Syrah. I had struggled with these grapes in the past. During the tasting, I narrowed in on them in my mind. I wanted to put my best performance forward. I thought about how much I had improved after the months of struggle. *Maybe I'll be a sommelier the next time they see me.* I held tight to the well-deserved confidence. I was getting in the zone.

As I was collecting a few things from my room for the trip, I glimpsed an envelope with my name on it on my desk. I opened it, and inside the card it said, "Don't lose your daydream." Katie had written me an inspirational note. She had drawn a picture of me popping a bottle of bubbles and her and Mater sitting at our kitchen table. She will never know just how much I needed that final vow of encouragement. I beamed while my eyes watered. I brought the card with me and began the two-hour drive to San Francisco to keep chasing my daydream.

I pulled into the Sir Francis Drake Hotel and was greeted by the attendant at the front. He asked how I was. Though I'm sure he was expecting a generic "fine" response, I blurted out that I was taking my certified sommelier exam the next day. After my random blabbering, he just looked at me for a moment. I know he had no clue what I was talking about, but he said, "You are going to do just fine." I don't know if he truly meant it, but his words stayed with me. Perhaps I would do just fine.

At the front desk, I noticed the name tag of the gentleman checking me in for the night. His name was Elgin. I thought it was such an interesting name, and I felt that I should've known why it was important. Then it hit me. I loudly exclaimed, "South Africa!" His head whipped up from the computer, and a quizzical look emerged on his face. I explained that his name was a wine region in South Africa. My outburst led me to explain the exam I was going to take the next day. As I walked away to my room, he told me I was going to do just fine. Elgin did two things for me that afternoon: he gave me that additional ounce of support and reminded me to crack open my notes on South Africa.

As I sat in my hotel room that evening, I shut the books and put away my notes. I decided I had done everything I could do. I was ready. I turned off the lamp and had visions of service swirling around my head.

I awoke to the song "I Can Go the Distance," from *Hercules*, which always seemed to give me a little extra belief in myself. I had come prepared for my pretest warm-up. I opened my final practice bottle of cheap sparkling wine without making a sound. I thought, *What the hell*, and took a big swig of bubbles and headed down to the banquet room to begin my day of examination.

I navigated my way to the area where we were to meet for a full day of testing. I saw men and women of all ages dressed in "somm"-looking outfits going the same direction as myself. We all exchanged nervous smiles, but the tension could be cut with a knife. I arrived at the banquet room and saw about two hundred other hopeful candidates.

As we all got settled, the master sommeliers leading the testing got up and introduced themselves. I was so impressed with their presence and achievements. Part of me deep down wished I could be up there one day. They outlined how the day would go. We would start with the written exam portion, followed by the blind tasting, and finish with service.

The pages of tests circulated table to table. The next thing I knew, they were telling us we had forty-five minutes and wished us luck. I flipped the cover page and went into autopilot. Question after question, I felt content with my answers. It was if I had muscle memory, having grilled facts for weeks without relent. The beginning was a simple warm-up; however, the test started throwing curveballs.

Midway through the test, I felt beads of sweat collecting at my brow, but then two of the next hard questions involved South Africa. One of the questions asked where Elgin was. I let out a chuckle thinking of Elgin at the front desk.

The other one hundred ninety-nine people feverishly taking the exam probably thought I was insane. The hour was up after what felt like five minutes. I didn't know if it was enough, but I had thrown everything I had at the exam. I couldn't think about it long because we were ushered out of the room so the master sommeliers could pour our blind wines.

As we all reentered the grand hall, familiar wine aromas filled my nostrils. I was absolutely terrified but wanted more than anything to get in front of the wines. Sitting back down, I was transfixed by the two wines in front of me. In my mind, I begged them to reveal their identities swiftly to me.

The master sommeliers told us to start tasting. Everyone lunged for their wines. As I reached forward, I heard the faintest laughter in the back of my mind. It was the laughter I had carried with me from Kyle during my first blind tasting. The memory found its way into my mind at my most defining tasting moment. I could either let it knock me off the path or let it continue to be my fuel for tasting success. I pushed the fear and doubt aside. I assured myself no one would laugh at me again.

Swirling the white wine in my hand, I analyzed the color, and it didn't have any defining character. Then I stuck my nose in the glass. My mind went wild. I had just smelled these same aromas. They were so fresh in my memory. I kept smelling, and the wine came into focus in my mind's eye. This wine had exactly the same smell as several Pinot Grigios I had smelled the previous day, I was almost certain. I continued to tear apart the wine. I tasted the wine to get the structure, and I knew I had my answer. All the puzzle pieces pointed to Pinot Grigio. It was my final answer. I wrote down "2014 Pinot Grigio from northern Italy."

Riding the wave from the white, I grabbed the red wine. I studied the dark ruby wine and gathered clues from the color. In smelling the wine, I was stunned. Not because the wine left my brain blank; rather, an unmistakable familiarity filled every inch of my mind. It was the exact kind of red wine I had been tasting the day before as well. The wine in the glass pointed to the same red-fruited, black currant, spicy, and meaty scents I had smelled at my last tasting. Could I have been given the exact same wines I was blinded on the day before? Regardless, I kept diving into the wine, and again, everything in my mind screamed a 2013 Syrah (Shiraz) from Australia. I wrote down my answer and handed in my answers with a mix of hopefulness and marvel at the coincidence of the situation.

The final leg of the examination was everyone's most dreaded. It was where many capable people failed. We were broken into groups to carry out our mock service for the master sommeliers. Now, when we were split up, everyone started to relax a bit and get to know each other.

The other ten people in my group and I gathered in the lobby. We waited to be called for our turn. We began the wine small-talk, and I met a few pretentious candidates. Then I met a girl with a warm smile and clearly not an ounce of pretention. I could tell she was my kind of friend. She introduced herself as Clare. We continued to try to put each other at ease.

Naturally, everyone began discussing the service feat in front of us. A middle-aged woman somewhat intruded into Clare's and my conversation. I could tell the woman was nervous and just needed to vent. She made it clear this was her second time taking the exam after failing previously. God, the thought of failing was sickening, but I knew it would be a reality for maybe half of us there. She began discussing her service portion from the failed attempt. At that point, I was half listening as I was trying to mentally prepare for my turn at bat. I caught the tail end of her story. She said they had asked her to give pairing suggestions for a meal of chorizo and clams.

"Can you believe that?" she exclaimed to all of us. "What the hell do you pair with chorizo and clams?"

I thought about it for a few moments, and I felt a Tempranillo from Rioja would be a successful match. I blurted out my suggestion, and a few other people listening in agreed.

Our turn was up, and we all proceeded into the room that could make or break us. Sparkling wine stations were set up around the room. At each table sat a master sommelier. The exam leader addressed us all and assigned everyone a table.

I was directed to a woman named Emily. She was the only one smiling. The leader told us all to go ahead and start. I confidently approached the smiling master sommelier. I was in autopilot, and I hit every checkmark of service in my head. I presented her the bottle. I initiated opening the bottle. I pleaded for the required whisper from the bottle. While doing this, I had heard several pops ringing out around the room and subsequent sighs of disappointment from the candidates. I glanced up as I removed the cork. For the briefest moment, my mind's eye saw Katie and Mater smiling up at me in our kitchen.

The bottle made a slight hiss, and I snapped back into reality. I continued with service, pouring champagne into all the glasses. Then I stood before Master Sommelier Emily to field the question portion of service. I asked her if I could assist in pairing wine with her meal. She said she would be having the chorizo and clams. My mouth dropped slightly open. Without missing a beat, I answered Tempranillo. I confidently suggested possible producers from Rioja. I shared why the pairing would work in detail. I had gone through this scenario not ten minutes before in my mind. She hit me with at least fifteen other challenging wine-related questions. I took them all in stride. Then, just like that, it was done.

We all congregated outside, and the banter began again. We had several hours before the masters would announce the results. The relief of being done intertwined with a feeling of uncertainty about the outcome. Chatting with a few other potential sommeliers, I wanted to share my chorizo-and-clam story, but a particularly know-it-all candidate monopolized the conversation. He interjected about the things he "almost" forgot to do during service, which would surely have led to a complete failure of the exam. His conversation raised questions in my mind. I mentally replayed my performance over and over. As he kept talking, uncertainty filled my mind.

At the exact moment I thought my head was going to explode, Clare walked by. Seeing my exit opportunity, I got her attention. I completely cut off the know-it-all and asked Clare if she wanted to go explore San Francisco. I could tell she needed to be rescued from the endless second-guessing conversations as well. She jumped at the idea, and we left all the stress, nerve-racking discussions, and uncertainty behind.

We had somewhat of an unspoken agreement not to speak about the day's events. I knew both of us wanted to escape the shallow comparisons of performance going on inside the lobby. As we walked outside and San Francisco's possibilities met us, I took a moment to take in the scene. I had just taken an exam the outcome of which could potentially change my life. I had a knot the size of Texas in my stomach. I was standing next to someone who I knew felt the same emotions.

We had four hours before the results would be announced. We could waste those four hours and be consumed by our own insecurities and doubt, or we could do something else. We looked at each other and resolved to keep walking and see where the day would take us. Instead of spending more time on meaningless test talk, we truly got to know one another. We spent those four hours talking about everything and nothing, walking through markets, visiting the sea lions, trying delicious food, and taking in the energy of the city.

We had both put each other at ease, and we knew, whatever happened, life was truly about connecting and sharing experiences.

The day was coming to a close, and the Sir Francis Drake was beckoning us back to hear our results. As we entered the lobby jam-packed with wannabe somms, the same nervous energy flooded back to us. We kept our newfound resolution to hold on to the value of relationships and the spontaneity of life. We made an unspoken vow not to let the results of one test change our outlook.

All two hundred of us funneled back into the banquet room. This time there were blank tabletops. The army of master sommeliers standing at the front held the pins and certificates for those who had passed. The main sommelier gathered everyone's attention. He delivered the traditional *thank you all for coming out*, the 54 or so percent pass rate, and other pieces of information I truly wasn't even comprehending due to my anticipation. He had a stack of certificates in his hands and a table of sommelier pins next to him. As he read the names on the certificates in front of him, my heart rate spiked.

Claire and I were sitting next to each other. We gave each other a final nod of support. I gazed downward yearning to hear the familiar sound of my own name. He called name after name. After each one, I felt my heart sink. After what felt like two hours, I noticed the minuscule stack of certificates left in his hands. He called another name, and then one certificate remained.

I looked down again, and that time it was in despair. I had accepted defeat in my mind, but I racked my brain trying to recall when the next round of testing would be. I made up my mind: I would just sign up again as soon as we were let out of the banquet hall.

Then the leader stopped to speak before saying the last name. He exclaimed the last certificate was reserved for the person with the highest score and the recipient of the Walter Clore Scholarship. I didn't even know it existed. As he said those things, a pang of jealousy ran through me; I would've given anything at that moment to be the name on the last piece of paper.

He called the name. Just like in the movies, everything went into slow motion. I looked up at Clare. She had a huge smile across her face.

He had called *my name*.

A master sommelier called my name to say I had achieved the highest score on the exam. I didn't have time to process what had just happened. I went from thinking I had failed miserably to realizing I had done better than I'd ever thought possible. I walked to the front in a state of shock. The pure feeling of elation running through my body was unforgettable.

As I returned to my seat, the leader said the final goodbyes and congratulations. I sat staring at my name on the certificate. However, a realization came to my mind: Clare hadn't passed. I almost didn't want to meet her eyes. I was disappointed for her and couldn't stand the thought of seeing her melancholy face. I looked up and saw something that deeply impacted me. She was still beaming.

When we caught each other's glance, she mouthed, "Great job." It wasn't a fake or empty gesture; she was truly thrilled for me.

Driving home, thoughts of the day's events flooded my mind. I had acquired a lot more than a piece of paper. I gained an appreciation for what we were capable of if we resolved it to be possible. I didn't know what to call the occurrences that had pointed me in the right direction throughout the exam. I wasn't superstitious, but it was magic. Life could be cruel, but I wanted to keep finding the magic. Even the most mundane things, like a guy named Elgin, Pinot Grigio and Syrah, and a Spanish specialty dish, had the power to change the course of a life for the better. Much like my journey up until that point, it was about so much more than wine.

When I turned the key to my house in Napa, I heard Katie and Mater waiting up for me. I had told her the good news while still in San Francisco. I opened the door. They were sitting in our kitchen, but this time Katie opened a bottle of sparkling wine for me. As we sipped on bubbles, I told her all the stories of the exam. I made sure she knew how her unwavering support had pushed me to keep going despite the odds. I hoped she understood just how instrumental she had been in my success in becoming a sommelier. The next person I needed to personally thank would be Pierre. My personal coach, defender, and wine confidant deserved my thanks. I was due to work the next day, but as a sommelier.

I headed into work the next morning with a mix of excitement and nerves. I was thrilled to be able to share my happiness with Pierre and several coworkers, but not sure how some would react to the news.

I stopped by Pierre's desk first thing to share my news. The pride beaming from his face was the best thing I could've hoped to see. Then, it was on to the rest of my coworkers. As usual, we all convened for our morning meeting in the bistro, led by David G. The whole team was there, among them Kyle and Andrew. I had already shared my news with Matt and David M., and I'd felt their genuine congratulations. As David G. conducted the meeting, I sat with my new pin wondering who, if anyone, would notice without my cluing them in.

He ended the meeting with a final announcement. Word certainly traveled fast, because David G. told everyone there was a new sommelier among them. He looked straight at me and said how proud he was. He assured me it was just the beginning of what I would do with wine.

There was a collective murmur of surprise, but congratulations from the majority. I surveyed the room, taking in the moment. I caught Kyle's and Andrew's expressions. The level of disbelief spread across their faces almost made me bust out laughing. But I had learned that laughing in someone's face wasn't something I appreciated all those months ago at my first blind wine tasting, so I resolved to keep letting my abilities with wine do the talking—though I couldn't help doing a small internal victory dance.

Wine Talk: What Does a Sommelier Actually Do?

It's an age-old question. Many people assume sommeliers sit around drinking all day. Some think it's a made-up title. Still others are both intimidated and confused by the word in general.

When I first achieved the title of certified sommelier through the Court of Master Sommeliers, the most difficult part was trying to put into words what I was. When I announced my news to friends and family, I was greeted with enthusiastic congratulations. Then came the questions of what exactly the title meant.

In the early days I would go off on tangents trying to relay to people what it all meant. I would start to see people's eyes glaze over as I went on about the studying involved, the testing, and the ways to utilize the wine skills professionally. After one too many lengthy explanations, I began to describe myself as a "wine girl."

Much like any career or vocation, titles rarely make a person. In the world of wine, it's important to be able to define what a sommelier is. However, a true wine professional doesn't need a title to make you appreciate, marvel at, and fall in love with wine.

How do you pronounce "sommelier"?

I have heard the word *sommelier* pronounced many, many different ways. If you can pronounce the word correctly, wine people will take you more seriously. Here is how you pronounce it: "somm-all-'yay."

This is a rough guide, but the biggest thing I want you to avoid is pronouncing the *r*!

What is a sommelier?

This question is becoming harder and harder to answer. The world of wine and its reach is expanding rapidly. It seems as though there are new ways every day to work as a sommelier.

I see the definition of a sommelier as broad and changing. The Court of Master Sommeliers roughly defines a sommelier as a wine professional who works on the floor of a restaurant to aid guests in the selection, understanding, food pairing, and service of wine. Along with these responsibilities, a sommelier must be proficient with every major wine region, grape variety, and producer in the world. This is a very restaurant-focused definition.

For me, a sommelier is anyone who is passionate about wine and works tirelessly to learn more and share the craft. With this base, a sommelier is someone who has passed the necessary examinations by the court, but after this, I believe how one uses their certification is subjective.

The way one feels they can share their gift of wine with the world defines a sommelier to me. I don't care if you work in a wine shop, at a winery, as a distributor or a writer, in the vineyards, as a winemaker, on the floor of a restaurant, or as a teacher. We are all sommeliers. We all share our passion for wine in our own ways.

What questions should I ask a sommelier?

A major goal for me is to have people gain confidence in their interactions with sommeliers at restaurants. Even if you know nothing about wine, you can still confidently interact with a sommelier. If you ask the right questions, you will get the right answers. My main three go-to questions are:

1. What wine in the X price range will go best with what I am eating?
2. What is a wine on the list you are most excited about for X price?
3. If I always drink [whatever you usually drink], what is a similar but new wine I could try for X price?

A skillful sommelier will be able to recommend a bottle of wine that will satisfy you and hopefully broaden your wine mind. The questions I recommend asking will undoubtedly lead to an even more fulfilling wine experience.

What are other jobs of a sommelier at a restaurant?

In the rough definition of a sommelier, a lot of the description had to do with the work of the sommelier during dinner service at a restaurant. However, there are even more roles of a sommelier in the restaurant setting.

In addition to being a resource for the guests, sommeliers should be a resource for all the other employees of the restaurant. This means they should be actively educating the staff in an engaging and encouraging way. The goal is to make sure everyone working at the restaurant feels comfortable and unintimidated by wine. Another huge aspect of the job involves the cellar. Keeping the wine cellar organized and accounted for is the less glamorous part of a sommelier's life.

The most vital role is to stay humble and hungry to learn more about wine. While sommeliers have the ability to make people feel inferior with their vast knowledge about wine, the true role of a sommelier is to make wine accessible, understandable, and a way to bring people happiness.

Are sommeliers really necessary at restaurants?

In the past, sommeliers were seen as intimidating or pretentious. Many restaurant patrons would even try to avoid having one visit their table. Some assumed sommeliers were present to try to trick you into spending more or buying a bottle you didn't truly want. Luckily, this perception of sommeliers is changing.

I see the relevance of a sommelier in a restaurant as someone to enhance your wine experience and thus the dining experience overall. Dining out is not simply about going out to eat. In today's world, people go out to eat to feel joy, share an experience with a loved one, or be elevated above the monotony of everyday life by what they eat or drink. A sommelier can use their intimate knowledge of the menu and every bottle on the wine list to orchestrate the best experience for you as possible.

Due to this fact, sommeliers are the storytellers, connoisseurs, and servers who have the potential to take a dining experience from great to sensational. Even for smaller wine lists, they are an indispensable part of a restaurant. They are passionate liaisons between the winemaker and the wine drinker, which makes them invaluable to the fullest enjoyment of wine.

10

Confidence Mixed with Wine

My life in Napa started feeling different after hearing the sweet sound of my name called as a certified sommelier. I walked taller through Inglenook. I was on the exact same level as everyone else, and it felt pretty damn good. I didn't want to simply sit on the sidelines anymore. I was ready to immerse myself in the wine world of Napa without a single reservation. Many people take a hiatus from the study of wine after the stress, hard work, and difficulty of preparing for the rigorous test. The last thing they want to do is to keep putting in endless hours of extra work with wine. I never was quite like most people; I doubled my efforts to learn more. I wanted to know everything. I desired all the knowledge I could get my hands on. Deep down, I knew I had to protect the legitimacy of the pin displayed on my jacket.

Along with continued studying, I felt like I deserved to have a bit more fun. The confidence I'd developed with wine had a way of intermixing with my social life. I became the Napa "yes" girl. If there was ever a function, a winery party, a chance to go out, I leapt at the opportunity to feel alive in the valley.

My chance arrived when I received an invite to the Raymond Vineyards Masquerade Ball. According to the crew at Inglenook, it was always the party of the year. The owner of the winery had quite the reputation for putting together parties like a scene straight out of *The Great Gatsby*. This ringleader of outlandish experiences was Jean-Claude Boisset. He was a famous *negociant* (a wine merchant) from Burgundy. I had only ever read about him in books. I could recite details about his activities in the wine world, but I was ready to get my head out of the books and into the real world. The night of the ball, I headed there with a few friends, and I wanted to stir up a bit of trouble. My golden mask shimmered as I sauntered onto the dance floor. The glass of bubbles running through my veins made anything possible on the dance floor.

I ended the night asking Jean-Claude Boisset to pour sparkling wine into my mouth. He just so happened to be in a life-size champagne glass. As the cool effervescence slid down my throat, I felt the spark I had been looking for. I wanted to keep it alive.

The next chance to live it up in Napa came in the form of a high school crab feed. Not exactly my first thought for a way to blow off steam on a Friday night, but a guy who frequented Inglenook invited me to be his date. His friends were teachers at the high school, and he guaranteed we would have a fun time. I took the bait and embarked on one of the strangest dates I have ever been on.

We arrived at the school, and I was by far the youngest in attendance as a guest and not a student. It was my date and myself in a sea of parents and grandparents. The feeling of wanting to escape the event as soon as possible disappeared as my date placed two drink tickets into my hand. I mean it was *two* drink tickets—how much damage could I do? Two Long Island iced teas later, I found out.

As we headed into the main gym for the crab feed, I needed food more than anything. There were cheerleaders at the entrance thanking us all for being there for the fundraiser. My Long Island–influenced mind seized an opportunity to make an entrance, of course.

I found the squad leader and asked if they could spell out my name as I walked through the doorway. She jumped at the chance to break the monotony and rallied some of the other girls together. My date couldn't hold in his laughter as I set the stage for the night.

All eyes turned toward the doors as "Give me a *K*! Give me an *A*! Give me an *R*! Give me an *A*!" filled the gym.

With my mission accomplished, I saw myself as the queen of the crab feed. The parents present no doubt disagreed with my self-proclaimed title. The parental stares intensified throughout the evening. I only ate one crab leg and drank my weight in Riesling. Naturally, I ended the night kissing my date at the end of the long red-and-white-checkered table.

The principal, sitting across from us, stared stunned and amused. My date's friends, wanting to extinguish the possible crab-feed scandal, hurriedly whisked us out of the gym. As we walked through the exit, I heard a "Give me a *K*" from the cheerleaders. One of the mothers abruptly silenced the squad. My last act of defiance was a very much cliché *Breakfast Club*–style fist pump as we turned the corner to leave.

A realization dawned on me when I awoke the next morning with a pounding headache. My two craziest nights out were spent surrounded by people in their forties. I needed an old Frenchman to pour champagne down my throat from a life-size champagne glass to feel a rush. I made out in a high school gymnasium after rallying a cheer squad to spell out my name. If these actions weren't a cry for me to make a change in my life, I don't know what would've been.

I started to look for other ways to fill the void I kept experiencing. I resolved it was time to start trying to find someone to share my life with. I had no desire to date anyone during the time of unrelenting sommelier prep. Since that chapter was over, I was ready to throw myself into finding a relationship. It was my last-ditch attempt to scratch the itch I couldn't ignore anymore. Trying to find love became my way to feel the electricity in my bones while avoiding future escapades in the valley.

As my hunt for love began, I realized I knew just about every eligible bachelor in town. I had forgotten just what a small and pastoral place it was. Coinciding with my dismay over my limited prospects, my mentor Pierre approached me with a holiday party invitation. In true Pierre fashion, he subtly hinted he was inviting a Master of Wine named Ted. He let me know he was single, and with a wink, he turned away telling me to make sure to be there. The matchmaking game was in motion, and I wasn't about to stop it.

I arrived at the party with extra mascara and bright red lips. I made the rounds meeting the guests at Pierre's house. I kept waiting to be introduced to the Master of Wine. I had no idea what he even looked like. To my disappointment, we all sat down to dinner and no Ted. As we settled in, the doorbell rang. I was seated facing away from the entryway, and I heard a British accent offer apologies for being late. The moment he spoke, I knew it was him.

He sat next to me, at the head of the table, and he introduced himself extending his hand. Immediately his kind eyes struck me. We were finally acquainted, and I had a few other realizations. He was certainly good looking, but definitely not in his twenties. I should've known a man of his status would have some age on him.

Everyone began peppering him with questions. Having a Master of Wine at the dinner party added a sense of novelty. There aren't many of them out there, and everyone was clearly impressed, myself included. When he began speaking about the wine he was tasting, I was entranced.

His eloquence, knowledge, and abilities with wine stunned me. They say you fall in love with someone at first sight. You don't need words, you just know. It's the initial physical desire people always talk about. With Ted, my mind fell in love that night. I had never felt attraction in that way before. My mind was completely head over heels. Nothing physical even mattered.

Since I didn't have the brain of a wine master, I resorted to much less academic methods of flirting. I turned my charm on. As the wine kept flowing, we began moving closer and closer throughout dinner. Pierre's love of Indiana Jones and Star Wars came out at dinner in the form of costumes being whipped out. Pierre decked Ted out in the full Indiana Jones costume, complete with whip. I found myself in Ted's arms to take a picture. The evening ended with "Indiana Jones" asking for my number. I wasn't about to say no to Indy.

The next morning, I received the most formal yet sweet text from him. I almost felt like I was reading poetry as he invited me for drinks. And so, Ted and I leapt into dating. Our relationship turned into a myriad of dates revolving around wine. I could listen to him talk for hours on end. I lusted for his words and expertise. Each time he would have me over to his apartment, he would cook and have blind tastings set up for me. After countless nights full of wine, conversation, and food, I completely fell for him.

In the past, I had notoriously never let myself fully give in to a man or a relationship. I needed something "special" to draw me in for more than a month or so. I figured there would be fireworks going off and I would have trouble even breathing around "the one." My love for Ted was nothing like what I expected. Wine and the sense of security drew me toward him.

I let myself go into cruise control. I grew comfortable with him. I trusted him with everything, and he became my own personal Master of Wine. He believed in my abilities with wine fiercely. He fed into my wine passion in undeniable ways. Funnily enough, my search to shake up and reinvigorate my life led me to complete stability with Ted.

The same stability I felt with Ted, I began to feel at work as well. I led tours, tastings, and events and guided people to fall in love with Inglenook and wine. I knew exactly what to expect from each day. My knowledge was more than enough for the wines I worked with day in and out. But I started to feel as if I wasn't growing anymore.

The sense of stagnation hit an all-time high in late March during my second year in the valley. I led a tour, and after it concluded, I felt nothing. All the times before, I had typically felt a rush of nerves waiting for guests to arrive, a feeling of achievement after, or at least a fascination with the people joining me on the experience. For the first time, the tour was monotonous and commonplace.

I fixated on the lackluster emotions for the rest of the day. I had strived so hard to move up at Inglenook, to become a somm, to gain the respect of those around me. It dawned on me while reflecting on the day's events—my dreams would cease to have meaning if I ever became merely satisfied with what I did. It nearly killed me, but in the days following those thoughts, I knew I wouldn't be able to stay at Inglenook. I loved Inglenook more than I ever imagined I would. However, I foresaw the admiration I had for the winery turning to resentment if I let my growth die there.

The thought of being there long enough to lose the unconditional love and pride for my work tore me apart. I knew what I had to do. I was approaching my two-year mark in the valley, and I resolved to make a serious change in the direction of my life. Despite being unsure what exactly it would be, I gave myself permission to start looking for what it could be.

The same soul-searching I did at the end of my time at UF filled my thoughts again. Perhaps I'd drunk the Court of Master Sommelier Kool-Aid, but I felt as if I needed to be in a restaurant, not a winery. Master sommeliers guided young sommeliers to work in restaurants. They advised that it would be essentially the only way to become a master sommelier. Something inside me kept saying I had to do it, that restaurant work would be my next challenge and way to keep evolving.

I racked my brain trying to decide which restaurant I wanted to work at in Napa or maybe in San Francisco, but I couldn't fight the feeling of wanting more. I did all I could to try to see opportunities for my aspirations in Napa. I shadowed at several restaurants for a sommelier position, but nothing quite felt right. As I scrutinized what my career would look like away from Inglenook, I started looking more closely at what my life outside of work had become in Napa.

My routine had become predictable. I ran in the morning, went to work, gave tours and tastings to people who all blurred together, had a few sips of wine with the rest of the staff in the bistro, and then visited Ted's or had him over or went out to one of my usual spots in downtown Napa. It was a perfectly good life. I was perfectly happy. I could've lived it for the rest of my life. I wouldn't have needed anything else but the beauty and simplicity of it all.

Something in the back of my head kept whispering *more*. Not in the sense that I wanted more money, happiness, friends, or excitement. *More* in the sense that I had more to discover and I needed to be more. I started searching for the way to be *more*.

New York City kept popping into mind. It had always been my far-off dream after being intrigued by the city when I was a freshman in college. Life had taken me down a different path, but my fascination with this long-lost vision was reawakened. Like clockwork, I would meet a guest from New York every day. When they said they were from New York, I felt my heart beat a little faster.

New York City was culturally and mileage-wise a world away from my wine nirvana. Each time guests from NYC would join my tours, I gravitated to them afterward. I found myself talking to them about the city, and my interest kept growing. Much like my visions of Napa in college, I felt the obstacles to make it a reality were unsurmountable. But of course, a sign was about to nearly slap me across the face.

It was a rainy day at Inglenook in late March. The guest traffic was slow, to say the least. I was scheduled to lead the tour at 11:00 a.m. for ten people. At eleven fifteen, no one had showed, and with this kind of weather it wasn't too surprising. Then, as we were ready to call it on the tour, two young girls hopped out of a car and began running in the rain across the courtyard. Everyone at the front watched them as they finally made their way through the grand entrance to the front desk. For some reason, their arrival filled me with an unexpected rush of serendipity, as though I was supposed to meet them.

They were both twenty-two, and needless to say, the median age was quite a bit higher with my usual day-to-day interactions. They asked if we did tours. Since our regular tour had been canceled, I offered to take them around. The front desk carded them, and once they paid and everything checked out, we began the rainy spur-of-the-moment tour. We immediately became fast friends, and I came to find they were from New York City. My fascination was clearly piqued.

At the end of the tour, we all headed into the tasting room in the caves of Inglenook. We discussed wine for maybe fifteen minutes, but then the conversation turned to getting to know each other. They were so curious about my lifestyle, how I found myself in Napa, and what living in the valley was like. I enjoyed telling them my story, and I loved seeing their eyes light up with the discovery of how I came to be the sommelier before them.

We talked about their goals and dreams, and I tried to get a better idea of what it was like to live in NYC. I had never gotten this kind of intimate look into what life was like in that famous city. They talked about its energy, the endless activities, and the myriad of different people living within the city limits. The more they talked about their home, the wider I could feel my mouth opening. I had only ever seen New York as an intimidating place, a place I probably would never be a part of. There were too many horror stories, too many failures there, too many dead dreams. They slowly started to shake my misconceptions of the city.

I stopped them midsentence and asked if they could see me living in New York City. I had never truly even asked myself if I would fit in there. We all stared at each other, and then their excitement hit a peak. They exclaimed I would be perfect for New York and how much of a wine city it was. They had a genuine excitement for the prospect of me living and working in New York. We finished my longest tour to date and exchanged Facebook requests. As they left, we mostly jokingly said we would see each other in the city when I moved there.

Something in me changed after that unexpected tour. The idea of trying my hand in New York was intoxicating. The wind of change I had been begging for seemed to be pointing me to the East Coast.

The two girls I spent the afternoon with weren't the only reason I made up my mind about New York. Rather, having expressed my desire out loud finally made it a possibility in my mind. Their confirmation of my ability to do it was merely an ember to help ignite the fire inside me. It seemed absolutely crazy that I had resolved to move to a completely new city within a single afternoon. But by the time I was pulling away from beloved Inglenook that evening, I knew I had to move to New York City to work in a restaurant as a sommelier.

Making up one's mind is a very dangerous thing to do. I hadn't told anyone yet of my plans or any desire to move. The only two people in the world who had a clue of what I was planning were the two New Yorkers I'd toured around Inglenook. I knew the first person I was going to tell. This whole journey had begun with my mom, and the next chapter would have to begin with her too.

I texted her the morning I was working on my résumé and preparing to reach out to every New York contact I had made through my wine tours in California. I wrote to her that I truly believed New York City was where I needed to be next. I told her I wanted to work in restaurants. I told her I had the same feeling I'd had two years before about Napa. I hit send, not knowing what to expect. This would most likely blindside her.

Her reply was three words. Three words I was avoiding asking myself. Three little words that could knock my newfound momentum completely off track.

She asked me, "Are you sure?"

Her response made complete sense. I had spent two years in Napa, and now I wanted to pick everything up *again*, drive all the way across the country *again*, and jump into a vast expanse of uncertainty *again*. I know she was just looking out for me and didn't want me to take a regrettable misstep.

In a way, her text turned my whole stomach upside down. Regardless, I texted her back all the reasons I felt my gut was right. I wasn't so much trying to convince her, but rather I was trying to reassure myself. The last thing I texted was a promise not to do it if she didn't believe in me.

The only thing she texted back was, "Do it."

When I read her text, I was transported back to our fateful lunch over two years earlier. The same feelings rushed back to me. I had complete confidence in my decision. I set out to create a way to follow my unlikely dream, once again.

Wine Talk: Producers to Know (and Drink) from the "Big Three"

Having the chance to visit vineyards around the world is a huge perk of studying and working with wine. Many of the wines I recommend tasting below I had the opportunity to taste firsthand from the people who made them.

One particular tasting journey took me to Siena, Italy, where I gallivanted throughout the vineyards of Tuscany. While in Siena, I ventured into a hole-in-the-wall wine shop. The husband-and-wife owners spoke broken English, but we managed to communicate. They recognized how genuinely interested I was in their wines. They brought me taste after taste and did their best to tell me the stories behind the wine. However, when we would all take a sip of wine, our facial expressions and reactions were the only communication we needed. Wine truly had its own language for us.

I encourage you to seek out new wine regions to explore, wines to try, and producers to appreciate. Combining wine, travel, and an open mind can create unforgettable moments. Even better, wine can always transport you back to them.

What are the producers I should try from California, and why?
One of the best things about wine is the fact that a wine can taste dramatically different based on how a winemaker chooses to grow the grapes and vinify them. *Vinify* is just a fancy name for turning grape sugars into our friend alcohol.

Branching out of your comfort zone of familiar producers is key to discovering amazing wines out there. Many people are used to Californian wine, but by trying more undiscovered producers, you can broaden your wine horizons. The following wines had an impact on me the first time I tried them. Hopefully, you will have a similar experience.

1. Dunn Vineyards: Napa Valley, Cabernet Sauvignon, $95–150

This wine is a splurge and a break from the "normal" Napa Cabernet Sauvignon. The winery purposefully make wines to age and develop in the bottle. It's not a wine with intense jammy fruit and an overly plush mouthfeel, but a more thought-provoking and complex wine overall.

2. Hanzell Vineyards: Sonoma Coast, Pinot Noir, $55–100

These wines represent some of the best Sonoma has to offer. The winemaker makes a point to represent the vineyards accurately. There is an elegance in the wines, while they also showcase the fruit-forward quality that the California climate brings to the wine.

3. Ravenswood: Lodi, Old Vine Zinfandel, $15–35

Gluttons for punishment obviously have a place in California. Affordable, big, high alcohol, and begging for you to indulge in every rich sip, this is Zinfandel exactly the way fans of the grape like it.

4. Tensley: Santa Barbara, Grenache Blanc blend, $35–45

ABC (anything but Chardonnay). This wine is a unique break from the myriad of Chardonnays coming out of California. Yes, California does have other options of whites besides Chardonnay and Sauvignon Blanc. This producer is quality minded and committed to planting the best grapes for his land, despite their lack of "fashion" or familiarity.

5. Masut: Eagle's Peak, Pinot Noir, $30–150

The winery you may have never heard of but should really put on your "to-drink" list. The wines are absolutely delicious and pure. Eagle's Peak is a vineyard area in Mendocino. The climate is cooler and more impacted by elevation and the ocean influence. The result is a distinctive glass of Pinot Noir with more freshness.

What are the producers I should try from Italy, and why?
Called Oenotria, meaning "land of the vine," every part of this enchanting country is riddled with vines. For producers here, I feel it's important to try different producers from different parts of the country. Although Sangiovese (from the Chianti region) is the most planted grape, there are so many other beautiful wines right at your fingertips. The following wines will also be readily available at your local wine store now that you know what to ask for:

1. Giacomo Conterno: Barolo, Nebbiolo, $150–900

If you have never tried old Barolo, and I mean *old* Barolo, you haven't lived. This producer is my personal favorite, and you can track down older bottles for sure. The winemaker is a traditionalist, and the wine is still sensational even after forty or fifty years in the bottle. The Barolo grape of northwestern Italy is Nebbiolo. The wine is worth the price for a special occasion. It presents layers and layers of flavor and will pair masterfully with any dish made with truffles. Treat yourself.

2. Venica e Venica: Friuli, Pinot Grigio, $20–40

"Truly delicious" and Pinot Grigio rarely go hand in hand. However, this producer is doing some very special things with the grapes of northeastern Italy. Bland, unexciting wines are far from what this producer has to offer.

They are one of my personal favorites for white wine from northern Italy.

3.   Il Secondo Pacina: Toscana (Tuscany), Sangiovese, $18–45

When one thinks of central Italy Tuscany naturally comes to mind. One could easily go for the Super Tuscans or big-name producers from Brunello di Montalcino. I want to go in a bit of a different direction. I was fortunate to visit a small wine bar in Siena, and the fantastic young couple who owned it truly opened my eyes. They poured me this wine from a small and family-run winery in the hills of Tuscany. It blew me away for the price.

4.   D'Angelo: Basilicata, Aglianco, $11–20

Aglianco has a special place in my heart. Maybe it's the name. Maybe it's the true and uncompromising character this wine carries with it. It's a serious wine for a not super intense price tag. The wine comes from the region of Basilicata in the southern part of Italy.

5.   Planeta: Sicily, Chardonnay, $30–45

The often-forgotten island of Sicily is a fantastic source of wine beyond just Marsala. The best part about this wine is you are familiar with the grape. You will be less intimidated but get the opportunity to try an excitingly different expression of the grape.

What are the producers I should try from France, and why?
France and Italy compete year after year after year for the top spot in annual wine production. Despite production or preference, France deserves our respect as a guiding light in the wine world. It is indisputable: France offers some of the most delicious and dynamic wines in the world. I could write a whole book about options, and *many* people have, but here are a few I hold near and dear to my heart:

1.   Huet: Loire Valley, Chenin Blanc, $30–60

This is probably my favorite white wine producer in the entire world. I had the opportunity to visit this winery in the Loire
Valley, though I almost completely missed my chance while
trying to figure out the bus system in French. However, making it there and tasting the luscious, focused, refreshing, and flavorful wine made me a believer in the power of Chenin Blanc.

2.   Château Biac: Bordeaux, Cabernet-Merlot blend, $50–150

I have said this once and I will say it again: knowing the love and passion
behind a wine intrinsically increases your love for a wine. My friend
Yasmina and her family are the ones behind the Château Biac wines.
Their dedication and hard work to create beautiful wines is unmatched.
Their wines are a more modern and understandable version of Bor-
deaux. If you can get your hands on several bottles, enjoy every sip.

3.   Lanson: Champagne, $39–89

Good champagne is easy to find, but good champagne that won't
break the bank is the real challenge. This particular producer provides
a delicious wine from the Montagne de Reims region of Champagne.
I had the chance to taste with the winemaker. By doing this and
having my parents join me, I fell in love with this wine even more.

4.   Château Margaux: Bordeaux, Cabernet-Merlot blend, $140–600

One of the most famous wines in the world is undoubtedly Château Margaux. Why shouldn't your lips get to taste this famous
wine? The price tag matches its worldwide renowned status, but
a special occasion could justify such a purchase. The best part of
the wine is its sheer power balanced by elegance. Many times, the

wines are described as an iron fist in a velvet glove on the palate.

5. L'Effet Papillon: Languedoc-Roussillon, Grenache blend, $10–15

This is the wine you can drink endlessly and never get sick of it. It's from a region you may not be familiar with too. The Languedoc-Roussillon is located in southern France. It's the least "French"-style wine on the list. However, it is darn tasty, and you will get addicted.

11

Searching for the Big Apple

I FOUND MYSELF IN AN ALMOST IDENTICAL situation to when I graduated from college. As before, I needed a job before I made the trek all the way back across the country, only this time I had something I didn't have before: I was a certified sommelier. Having the title gave me a sense of comfort. I assumed the search would require far less effort.

With my head up in the clouds, I thought hundreds of restaurants in New York could use a sommelier like me. I revamped my résumé and opened up Gmail. I wrote up a generic inquiry letter to restaurants indicating I was a passionate sommelier from Napa. I did my research and found thirty or so restaurants I thought looked like a solid enough start. I fired off emails to wine directors, managers, and owners. After a full day of hunting, I sat back waiting for the interested emails to roll in.

After an hour with my eyes glued to the inbox, I figured the time difference was my problem. Everyone in restaurants was working and had no time to answer me yet. My head hit the pillow that evening with thoughts of a job offer from a fancy New York City restaurant waiting for me in the morning.

I leaped out of bed the next morning to check my email. I saw a hefty number of responses and felt excitement rising up from my gut. I opened each email with a hopefulness.

No, no, no, and no.

At least with my inquiry to Napa wineries, they had let me down gently. New York certainly had no time for a young sommelier with "cute" winery experience. A thought dawned on me: *Maybe my magic has run out.* But if the previous two years had taught me anything, it was I could handle the ups and downs of the journey. I decided to take another angle at the New York beast. Being in the "adult" world for the past two years, I'd learned it's all about being well connected. You always have to know somebody on the inside, and it seemed like an absolute necessity in this case.

Two people came to mind who had a small chance of propelling me into the New York wine scene. A guest during one of my tastings had expressed that she just *had* to connect me with her master sommelier friend. Months earlier, when this happened, it didn't seem like something I really needed to follow up on, but at this point, it couldn't have been more imperative.

I emptied every purse and all my work-outfit pockets until I found her business card. I emailed her about my plans to move to New York and how much I would love to be connected with her New York–based friend. Ten minutes later, I had my response, and this time, *success!* She gave me her friend Brian's email and wished me luck. I was on the trail. I simultaneously sent him a greeting email and reached out for his help. My boldness shone through, and I saw it as a New York warm-up.

Radio silence from Brian.

My next potential saving grace was Ted. Being a Master of Wine came with certain connections. Ted had regularly spoken of his many wine experiences after he visited New York. I knew he might know someone in the city willing to consider me for a job. By reaching out in this way, I would have to do something I was dreading—I would have to tell Ted I was leaving Napa and possibly never coming back.

Ted invited me over for dinner around the time I was planning to tell him about New York. He challenged me to the usual invigorating predinner blind tasting. Fixating on the wines in front of me, I almost forgot the news I needed to share with him. After I made my guesses and he plated dinner for us, I prepared myself to drop the bomb. I let him know I had some unexpected news. He had a completely quizzical look on his face.

I didn't sugarcoat it or give a long-winded explanation. I said I'd made up my mind to move to New York City in two months. I paused for his reaction. I could see the confused look turn into one of disbelief. Seeing it slowly hit him that I would be leaving was heart-wrenching. It hurt more than I imagined it would. I wished I could stay with Ted in Napa forever while still chasing after my wine dreams, but I had made my decision and there was no turning back. I noticed the sides of his eyes moisten. At that moment, a feeling rose from deep inside me, and I realized there was a real love between us.

We were sitting in silence, both being flooded with unspoken emotions. Then Ted suddenly shook off the disbelief and sadness in his eyes. He threw on a fake smile and proceeded to find out my plan. With my growing excitement in my plans for the future, his face grew heavy. After dinner and sharing my next grand adventure, it sank in there was no convincing me to stay.

He walked me to the door and assured me he would do everything in his power to help me succeed. He kissed me on the forehead. Every move he made had a bittersweetness attached to it. I hugged him, and we almost couldn't let go. When we did, I took a step back and turned to leave. I spun around as the door closed. Staring at the door, I whispered under my breath, "I'm in love with you."

I woke the next morning and let feelings of doubt creep into my mind after my evening with Ted. I couldn't let them linger, because the email I had been yearning for cleared away any thoughts of turning back. Brian, the master sommelier, emailed me back. I could tell he was intrigued and at least pleased to "meet" me. He asked me a few additional questions about what I wanted out of New York. I had to ask myself those questions and search for what I truly did want. He ended the email by letting me know he would help me out, providing me the crack in the door I wanted to throw open to reach New York.

I wasn't too keen on having all my chips in one bag, but no one in New York would give me the time of day, and I hadn't heard from Ted in a while. I understood he might not have wanted to jump at helping me find a way to leave Napa, but a few days later, he emailed with a potential option. He admitted his contacts in restaurants weren't vast. His help came in the form of offering to connect me with a sommelier who had hosted a dinner for him and other Masters of Wine in New York a few months previously.

I didn't know any restaurant somms in New York, and the introduction appealed to me very much. I thanked him profusely, and I marveled at Ted's selflessness to help me achieve my goal. He hooked us all up with an introduction email, and my hypothetical door inched open ever so slightly. By the end of the day, I had a master sommelier in my corner and a potential contact in Danielle from a restaurant called White Street.

I went about my day-to-day Napa life but felt the deadline I had given myself moving closer. Just as I was starting to lose faith in Brian and Danielle, they both emailed me on the same day. Brian wrote to let me know he had reached out to a friend of his who ran the wine program at a prestigious restaurant in the city. He was transparent with the fact that all he could do was make the introduction and let things go where they may. Brian assured me that Jeff knew about me and my desire to work in restaurants. Jeff was the wine director at a restaurant near Gramercy Park called Maialino. I realized this Jeff had the potential to provide me a one-way ticket to New York. My heart was full of gratitude toward Brian, who could've ignored my initial email upon receiving it.

Danielle's email also sparked my hope for my quest. She was kind enough to even reply to some random girl. She answered Ted's introduction email with excitement to possibly meet me when I made it to the city. I didn't just need a friendly contact; I needed a job. I decided to make it crystal clear that I was in the market for a job. Same as two years ago, I wasn't about to just take off into the sunset without at least a job to gallivant to. I pushed harder about the prospects of working at White Street.

As if history were repeating itself, I had two career prospects, a timeline I was determined to meet, and an unbreakable hopefulness for the future.

Danielle and I continued a bit of back-and-forth emailing, and it was becoming clear there wasn't much in terms of a job she could offer me. As despair started rearing its ugly head, everything took a huge turn. An email from Jeff at Maialino popped up in my inbox. He indicated Brian had reached out, and he would be interested in speaking with me about possible job opportunities. His note was short and sweet but included his phone number and told me to call around 3:00 p.m. his time that day. With thoughts of the future swirling in my mind, I was reminded of the past. I relived the fateful call with Inglenook. I wondered if the call with Jeff had the potential to create a new path for me.

At exactly three o'clock that very afternoon, I called Jeff. I wanted to avoid seeming overzealous, but I doubted it would be possible. He picked up after what seemed like ten minutes of ringing. The phone interview commenced with his slightly uninterested hello and my overenergetic greeting. He inquired about my plans, my restaurant experience, where I saw myself in five years. He hit all his bases as an interviewer, and I offered somewhat generic responses. I felt myself drowning in my own preplanned answers to his questions. I could hear his voice lose interest with each response. I realized the only thing that ever carried me to new opportunities was my passion and authenticity. I had to get real and see where it landed me, or I would never see my new direction come to light.

During his following questions, I let my guard down. I reiterated that I had no restaurant experience, but I would do anything just to be close to people and wine. I dove into my "five-year plan," which actually didn't quite exist. I knew my plan for living and made it into a neat five-year package. I shared with him the light I yearned to create in people's eyes, my hunger to learn more about wine, and my pursuit to use my unlikely passion to affect the world in my own small way.

After finishing my last-ditch attempt to land the job, he paused, and I could tell he was ruminating something. I wondered if my unique take on my wine industry goals was too much. I mean, I was dealing with a realistic New Yorker on the other end of the phone. As I prepared for the worst, his voice rang back in. He said he had an offer for me.

I waited anxiously to hear the position he wanted to extend to me. I longed for him to invite me to join his team as a sommelier. I filled with elation as he told me he wanted me to work at Maialino, though his tone made me think there was a catch.

He offered me a position as a food runner. He assured me it was a start, and after getting acquainted with the restaurant I would have a chance to work as a sommelier. I wasn't sure what a runner was. If it led to me being a somm in New York City, I didn't care. Much like my Inglenook decision, I seized the job, regardless of prestige or what I was going to be paid. I decided to figure out everything else along the way.

Jeff enthusiastically outlined my next steps to accept the position. I can't remember a word he said. My brain kept screaming I would be a New York sommelier. He ended by telling me he would see me in New York. My heart fluttered. The giant list of uncertainties laid out before me had an invigorating effect on me. There were so many reasons to be afraid, but none of them could touch me.

I officially had a job waiting for me. As my next steps fell into place, I knew the time had come to start telling everyone of my plans. Aside from Ted, Katie and my coworkers would prove the most difficult to tell about my plan to move back across the country. Katie and I relied on each other so much, and I was horrified to imagine she might think it would be easy for me to simply desert her. Regardless of her reaction, the time came to sit her down.

Tough news has a way of sounding more manageable with a touch of booze. I invited Katie to grab a drink, and as we sipped on the tasty sherry, I said I had to tell her something. Much like Ted, a questioning disposition firmly took hold of her face. I let her know everything happening in my life and my decision to go. Of course she didn't want me to leave, but the time for decision making was long gone. Her protests showed me how much she cared, and all I could tell her was I had to do it. We ended the night by recalling the start of our friendship in the hotel lobby and how many memories the valley had given us.

My last month moved along swiftly, and I had two weeks before my time in Napa would end. Inglenook deserved to know my plans. I had to give my two-week notice. I must've approached David, merely to rush away, several times over several days. I had started my unlikely journey with him. Something felt so absolute about telling him first about my quest to experience New York. It was the final puzzle piece of leaving Napa.

Finally, I asked if he had a few minutes after work to sit down with me. He agreed, and at the end of the day, we sat down in the bistro, where he introduced me to Inglenook two years earlier. Before I even spoke, a highlight reel of all my times in the bistro flew before my eyes. The room held some of my most cherished memories. He looked at me in the way I had hoped. He said he was wondering when this day would come. Much more like a dear friend than a boss, he told me he had enjoyed watching me grow there and said he knew I had to keep going.

The two days of a job you never forget are the first and the last. After the fastest two weeks of my life, my last day arrived. Nostalgia overtook me, and I questioned myself the whole day. There was no turning back, but it didn't stop me from wondering what might happen if I stayed.

As I went about the day, I experienced my mental "lasts." I had my last lunch with all my coworkers, who had become like family. I poured my last sips of wine for guests visiting Inglenook. I walked a little slower during the last times I walked through the halls of the historic château, thick with the rich smell of wine. I certainly didn't waste my last day. I absorbed everything I loved about Inglenook, as if to never lose its presence.

Everyone gathered in the bistro, as usual, for our postwork glass of wine. My work family took turns sharing a toast to me. My eyes watered more and more after each person shared what my time there meant to them. Their words solidified their belief in me. They may have believed in me more than I even believed in myself.

When my turn to speak came I shared that I never expected to love a place or the people surrounding me as much as I did. I made sure they knew my unbreakable passion for wine wouldn't exist without them. We all clinked glasses, and the final chapter of my Napa life closed. I finished my wine and savored every bit. I waved a final goodbye as I walked away through the caves for the last time.

As I made way to leave for good, I noticed a private event was being set up in the main entrance of the château. A violinist was preparing to entertain the guests during their dinner. She and the other members of the band were setting up next to the grand staircase. As I approached them to make my way up the stairs, the violinist caught my attention. We exchanged pleasantries, and she asked if I was guest or if I worked there. For the first time, I answered that I used to work at the winery.

I let her know it was my last day, and it had been one hell of ride working at Inglenook. My voice broke ever so slightly, and I could tell she noticed what the place meant to me. On my first step of the staircase, I turned back and told her I was moving to New York to be a sommelier. She looked up at me and said I would do just fine, as though she knew my uncertainty toward the future. The kindness of strangers never ceases to amaze me. I graciously nodded and kept climbing the stairs.

As I started to reach for the back door to leave with the thought of leaving my beloved Inglenook sinking in, I heard a familiar melody ring out. Frank Sinatra's "New York, New York" filled the château. The song filled every ounce of me and pushed me forward to my next chapter. I pushed the door open but turned back as the song was hitting the high notes. I mouthed *thank you* to the violinist. I left Inglenook with "New York, New York" ringing in my ears and my time there etched on my heart.

Wine Talk: Wine Evolution

Wine's evolution can be cultural, technological, or climatic, in the vineyard. These are a few examples showcasing wine's vast affinity for change. Wine will continue to change as people, technology, and weather patterns change. Thus, the opportunities for the study and appreciation of it are endless.

More so than wine's evolution, I enjoy seeing people evolve with it. I had my first real chance to witness people's growth during a twelve-week course I taught on wine. I was able to experience a group of students growing with wine, consistently, each week. Their confidence, intrigue, and knowledge expanded immensely. What most struck me was how at the end of the class people expressed their desire to continue studying wine.

Having a firm grasp on the areas in which wine can go through the most change is vital to its comprehension. However, understanding wine's nature of development and experiencing your own growth in tandem with it is the ultimate wine evolution.

How is wine culturally changing?

Even in my time working with wine, I have seen a shift in interest and a growing desire to learn by many people, especially younger people. The most profound impact wine has on our current culture is its ability to capture the intrigue of bystanders. Culturally, wine is transforming from being perceived as being off-limits and pretentious to more mainstream and approachable. Moreover, social media, Netflix specials, and reality TV are glorifying sommeliers and wine professionals. This is leading the growing intrigue as well.

In my experience, wine is a beverage that can inspire a genuine fascination in the taster. From once being thought of as an unattainable or hard-to-understand beverage, I notice it is shifting to being something younger generations are fully embracing. Certain statistics show millennials increasingly purchasing and enjoying wine from year to year and wanting to learn more fully about it. The changing perceptions of younger generations are most certainly changing the way society views and consumes wine.

Is the popularity of becoming a sommelier going up?

The only way to answer is with my personal experience of trying to help people get into wine. The number of people seeking guidance for certification continues to rise. Thus, the answer is undoubtedly yes. There is a huge push by people in "unfulfilling" or "boring" jobs to begin the journey into wine.

The key factors influencing a spike in sommelier popularity are documentaries, TV shows, and the "glamorous" lifestyle associated with wine. Whether the sex appeal of it all is true, more and more people desire to break into the mysterious and alluring world of wine.

The popularity of becoming a sommelier can also be measured by how many people are attempting to pass their certifications through various educational providers. The main three are the Court of Master Sommeliers, the Wine and Spirit Education Trust, and the Sommelier Society of America. Statistically, all the educational outlets have recorded increases in their student numbers and demand for their programs.

Are all wineries using more technological methods for winemaking?

Once the technology of temperature-controlled fermentation and cultured yeasts arrived in the 1970s, wine quality was much easier to control. *Cultured yeasts* refers to laboratory yeasts, or yeasts that were created to achieve a certain finished wine consistency after fermentation. Being able to more easily monitor temperature and yeasts helps producers make more consistent, controlled wine.

The more fascinating part of wine technology concerns the opposite end of the spectrum. Producers across the globe are trying to renounce wine "technology" as much as possible. They see the technological methods in winemaking as destructive to a wine's authentic nature.

One example I can provide concerns a wine from Spain made by a man named Daniel Ramos. Although he has yeasts, temperature control, and stainless-steel tanks at his fingertips, he chooses to make wine without using any of it. His winery is located in Castilla y León (a wine-growing region in north-central Spain), and his goal is to let his wines express this region fully.

He takes his organically grown Garnacha (the Spanish name for Grenache) grapes, slightly breaks them down manually to obtain the juice, and ferments the juice in an amphora, an ancient clay vessel. By using the inert (meaning not contributing any flavors to or influencing the wine) vessel and natural yeast on the outside of the grape skins, the wine is as natural as it can come. Many producers see making wine in this way as the most expressive of the particular grapes and where they are grown.

Thus, with expanding wine technology, there can be greater ease in creating a bottle of wine. From the growing, harvesting, sorting, pressing, fermenting, and bottling of the grapes, there is the potential to have complete control. However, wine purists will continue to denounce the degree of control that technology can provide.

What is climate change doing to grape growing?

Climate change is having a definite impact on vines around the world. A lot of people wonder whether or not the gradual temperature increases are having a negative or positive effect on vineyards. Instead of looking at grape growing on a broad scale, the best way to digest climate change is to look at its impact on a small scale. By focusing on a couple of well-known wine regions, we can illustrate the effect of climate change.

Overall, the impact of climate change is more positive than negative when it comes to vineyards. The best examples of regions benefiting from the slow temperature increase are the famous regions of Germany and Champagne. These regions are examples of growing sites with typically marginal climates. *Marginal* means the conditions, which are very cold or have extreme growing conditions, make growing grapes difficult. Thus, for regions like Mosel in Germany, the grapes have a greater risk of being underripe and creating thin, lackluster wines. The greater assurance of proper ripeness brought on by a warming climate means a higher chance of better-quality wine.

In speaking with several Mosel winemakers, the gradual temperature increases have affected the past fifteen or so vintages. In these years, Mosel has seen better, more consistent vintages on the whole, compared to the decades before this.

In terms of Champagne, their whole winemaking culture revolves around the lack of ripeness in their grapes. This is because grapes with less inherent ripeness are perfect for sparkling wine. So, along with a greater consistency in ripening, champagne is beginning to experience a slight change in the overall character of the wines. One can generalize more fruit character, and a slightly less bracing acidity is evident in the wines.

Are more producers trying to be organic?
Compared to the 1960s, '70s, and '80s, there is much more emphasis in the wine world on sustainability. Producers are looking to be more socially responsible and enhance the land rather than destroy it. There is also more call from consumers for organic wines.

They also realize many wine drinkers have discerning palates and won't respond as favorably to mass-produced subpar wine with negative impacts on the environment. Whether it's a way to sell their wine, grow better quality grapes, or invest in the environment, the tides are changing.

What can be said is, as a whole, there is a mindset based on the quality of grapes over quantity. This mindset, coupled with growing social awareness, has decreased harmful pesticide usage, and more natural vineyard management techniques are being used. Hopefully, this trend continues, leading to better wine for us and the environment.

12

New York, New York

WITH MY VISIONS OF NEW YORK on the horizon, I decided to make a pilgrimage to the heartlands of European wine country. I had taken two weeks to explore the famous wine regions I had studied for months. I ached to touch the ground and meet the people who made the wines that lit my mind on fire. I spent my travels going from Champagne to Bordeaux, Rioja to Tuscany, and wine-centric places in between. My love for wine increased on my trailblazing European trek. I truly believed it could take me anywhere. I navigated the foreign countries alone, and when I arrived back in the US, I was unafraid of my solo drive across the country and to take up residence in New York.

Anyone I shared details of my cross-country trip with was petrified for me. I didn't have time or energy for fear. The guiding mindset I had adopted was one of always moving forward. Fear can paralyze people. I resolved to move forward, and New York was waiting. It took me four days, five audiobooks, thousands of fleeting thoughts, and copious pit stops to finally pull into my parents' driveway. It seemed like only yesterday the same car had pulled out of the driveway of my Jacksonville home speeding toward Napa.

As always, my parents were waiting for me. Now it was my turn to inspire them with my own travels for and with wine. They had a bottle waiting for us, but I told them I had something else in mind. On my first stop in Paris, I purchased a bottle of wine I envisioned myself drinking with my parents. I bought it and carefully transported it across Europe. For me, it was more than just a bottle of wine, it was a reminder of my parents. I loved having it with me, even though at times a few less pounds would have been favorable.

Opening the bottle of wine, decanting it, and pouring it for us all provided a backdrop for my tales. I shared the details of the 1997 bottle of Caronne Ste. Ghemme wine from Bordeaux. It was my turn to guide them through the five Ss they had taught me years previously. I felt like I had become who I was truly meant to be as I presented my parents with the wine.

I explained that the wine had taken on a mahogany color after years of subtle oxygen exposure through the cork. I instructed them to gently swirl the wine, to wake it up after years in the bottle. I guided them through the unfamiliar, layered, and rustic bouquet the wine had developed over time. We all took a sip, and I communicated how to feel the mellow and complex nature of the wine on their palates compared to the young Napa Valley Cabernet Sauvignons they were used to. We savored every taste of the wine; I savored the chance to show my parents the knowledge I had worked tirelessly to achieve.

Sipping wine and reliving my trip with my original wine heroes felt sensational. I truly did become my parents. I imagined this was how they had felt sharing wine with me upon returning from Napa. If I loved something, I had to share it.

Two days later, the morning of my move to New York arrived, and I found myself in the same situation. My mom was in the driver's seat, and all my possessions were loaded up in the back. I thought about how different I felt compared to my move to Napa. I was stronger and more driven than before. I promised myself my goals of wine were in reach and to stay focused. I resolved to keep my head in the books and not to let New York distract me. I was convinced the city would have no effect on me. I intended for nothing to detract from the success I so desperately wanted.

Once again, the small details, in my mind, like housing and being alone in a new city, were afterthoughts. Craigslist saved my life once again with finding a place to live. I was set to live in a five-story walk-up with two boys in the East Village. This had "sitcom" written all over it. My mom stuck around to help me settle in. Then we found ourselves at the hardest part, again. We had to say our goodbyes. We weren't in pastoral Napa anymore. She must've seen it as her throwing me to wolves, but even the ever-intimidating New York couldn't dull her belief in me.

I didn't have much time to realize the fact that I was essentially alone in the city, as I was due to be at Maialino first thing the next morning. I bought all new black slacks and crisp button-down shirts. I assumed they would want me to look the part of a sommelier while I did my "runner" work. I believed in no time I would be living the sommelier dream.

I walked the fourteen blocks to the restaurant and breathed in my new city. There was something intoxicating about everything along the walk. I had the sensation that everyone was so alive. High off the emotions building inside me, I reached the front door to the restaurant and excitedly flung it open. I greeted the hostess, beaming. I told her I was there to meet with HR and begin work as a sommelier. Her disinterested look hinted to me that I was far too thrilled to be there.

She pointed for me to have a seat in the lounge and wait. I took a seat and gazed around wide-eyed at the place where I would come into my own as a sommelier. A younger-looking server approached me and introduced herself as Grace. I thought how much I needed some grace at that very moment.

We engaged in small talk, and she welcomed me. She asked what I would be doing with Maialino. I let her know they were starting me out as a runner, but I was sure to say I was a sommelier. She gave me a look as if she knew something I didn't. She looked me dead on and said I had an uncommon spirit about me. As I was taking in the compliment, her next words took me by surprise. She warned me not to let them kill it. I attempted to understand what she meant by "them," but HR arrived and gathered me up for paperwork.

I learned what Grace had meant on my very first day and subsequent days after. I quickly came to realize what a runner was. I had achieved a position at the absolute bottom of the barrel, *again*. I wasn't allowed to touch a wine bottle, let alone address a guest. Not to mention, of the coworkers who even acknowledged me, they were far from welcoming.

I found myself clearing and resetting tables, running food, and doing pretty much every restaurant job no one else wanted to do. I had no clue what a double was before working at Maialino. It was a way of saying I worked two shifts with minimal breaks in between. Despite all of it, I heeded Grace's advice. I wouldn't let them take my spirit.

I made sure Jeff knew how badly I wanted to be on his wine team. He wasn't quite the supportive and inspiring boss I had hoped for. I tried to befriend the sommeliers on staff. I answered every question in regard to wine at preshift staff meetings. I even nailed a blind wine at one of the meetings, causing surprise but not the respect I so desperately wanted. Even in my tireless efforts to be more than just a nameless, voiceless runner, several weeks passed with little headway. All my fellow coworkers seemed convinced there was a long line of potential sommeliers for the team before me.

Regardless of what was happening at Maialino, I still had my resolve to become a better sommelier each day. I heard through coworkers that a wine bar called Corkbuzz offered blind tastings in the early evenings. It was right up my alley, and I needed to stay sharp.

On one of my nights off, I decided to go try my hand at a flight of blind wines. Since I knew next to no one in my new city, dressing to impress wasn't on my radar. I threw on some gym clothes and walked to Corkbuzz from my apartment. I grabbed a seat at the end of the bar and realized I should have tried slightly harder to dress up. I looked out of place in the chic bar. When the respective red and white wines were placed before me, my thoughts of vanity disappeared. As I analyzed my last blind wine, I noticed the man next to me continuously glancing over. I thought the out-of-place girl in gym clothes smelling and spitting out wine wouldn't have to worry about guys distracting her. I was wrong.

He asked me what I was doing. His question led to him and his buddy sharing their outrageously expensive bottles of wine with me. I drank Grand Domaine de la Romanée-Conti, and I thought I could die and go to heaven. At the end of the once-in-a-lifetime wine experience for me, they invited me to go drink more iconic wine at a friend's shop. I exhausted every reason in my mind to say no, and something told me to just do it. That's how I found myself sipping on Dom Pérignon, Château Margaux, and my personal favorite, Rubicon, in gym clothes on a random Monday evening.

I came to find out the high rollers were Goldman Sachs investors. Not a single bottle they opened was under five hundred dollars. I ended the night being dropped off at my house by Marc, the one who inquired what I was doing with all my wine earlier in the night. We kissed good-night. I glided up my five flights and thought, *So this is New York.*

Still high off my surreal wine experience the night before, I was smiling, polishing silverware in the kitchen. Things were beginning to look up. There was a glimmer of light in my role with wine in the city. As I stared at my reflection in the spoon, one of the head sommeliers on the team approached me. I thought perhaps Kathy was coming to share something about wine with me. I had tried to engage her several times in previous weeks. I thought maybe she could act as somewhat of a mentor to me. She never quite gave me the time of day and knew my rank in the scheme of things. I saw her coming up to me as a sign that maybe my luck was changing.

Kathy came up close to me, and I opened my mouth to say hello, but she immediately spoke. She told me the wine community in New York was a very small place and she knew I was telling people I was a sommelier at Maialino. She made sure I knew to watch out in this town because a lot of people didn't make it. I had to visibly shake off my disbelief over what was happening.

There I was, a sweaty runner, bending over a dishwasher, polishing silverware. She stood before me in a distinguished outfit, freshly polished wine glasses in her hand.

I assured her there was some kind of mistake. I didn't want to cause any trouble. I made sure she knew I only ever said I worked at Maialino, and I was a certified sommelier. I apologized if I had created confusion. I felt myself sinking into the steam of the dishwasher. I was motionless.

The only thing she said was, "You're not a sommelier."

She began walking away. My heart wouldn't let me stand silent.

I objected by saying, "Yes, I am."

My statement made her turn back and say, "You aren't a sommelier, don't forget that."

I felt a stinging heat rush over me, and this time not from the dishwasher's boiling water spray. Kathy's words cut me so deeply, I physically ached. All my hard work, everything I had been through, my love for wine were all discredited by her. *You're not a sommelier* repeated in my head until I thought I was going to be sick. I let the dishwasher's steam cover my face to mask my visibly watering eyes.

I left the restaurant late that night after a double. On my usual path home, I noticed myself limping. I felt the full impact of blisters after spending fourteen hours on my feet. The skies opened up, and I felt the drizzling rain on my face. The streets were empty at that hour, and I gave in to my pain.

I cried. I cried over my opposition at work. I cried over the fear I might never see the day of being a sommelier in the city. I cried over the thought that maybe I wasn't meant for this. The next day my heart ached, and I prayed I hadn't made the biggest mistake of my life. Maialino was far from what I'd imagined. My only option was to move on. I could get knocked down, but I would be damned if I stayed down.

The first thought that crossed my mind was to email Danielle. The last time we had spoken I was telling her of my position with Maialino.

This time I had to get her to meet me and get her advice. I was so lost and needed anyone to give me some semblance of a guiding hand. I reached out to her and let her know I was in the city. I made sure she knew I really wanted to meet with her. I wished she could negate the pain Kathy had inflicted on me. I wanted someone on my side more than anything, especially in a city where the weak don't survive.

On the day we settled upon, I walked from my apartment in the East Village to Tribeca to meet her at White Street. It wasn't a job interview, but I was still nervous. Danielle was a wine director at a high-class, fancy restaurant, and I was a lowly runner. New York had a way of putting me in my place. Regardless, I wouldn't let my Maialino experience destroy my spirit. I wouldn't dare let them win.

I reached the White Street entrance, and I willed myself to restore the hope that brought me here in the first place. I pushed through the doors to find a classy 1920s'-style design. There were rich leather booths and dark, sexy colors everywhere. The restaurant was straight out of a movie.

A hostess was scurrying about and asked what I wanted. After letting her know I was there to meet Danielle, she made me wait by the entrance. The wall-to-wall wine cellar nearby caught my eye. I almost had my face pushed up against the glass to take in all the iconic wines before me. As I surveyed the selection, I saw someone approaching from the reflection in the glass. I turned around to see a beautiful woman walking toward me. I was immediately captured by the energy she was radiating. I was caught off guard. I was expecting Danielle to be some frumpy old woman. The person who walked toward me was the furthest thing from that.

I extended my hand to introduce myself, and she let me know she was a hugger. We embraced, and I felt I had made my first real friend in New York. She guided me over to the bar and told me to have a seat. I felt like I was meant to be there. I grabbed a barstool, and she poured us two glasses of water. She sat next to me, and I had another rush of nerves, this time not knowing where at all it came from. She told me to tell her all about my European wine travels and how I liked New York. I started in on some of the highlights of my travels. I thrived on her every reaction to my stories. I generally liked talking to everyone, but I genuinely liked talking to her.

She wanted to know all about Maialino. I felt like then was as good a time as ever to share the events that had transpired a few days earlier. As I was telling the story, she reached out for my hand to reassure me everything would be okay. I needed that more than she would ever know.

We had been talking for thirty minutes, which seemed to fly by. The rest of the staff were gathering for their preshift meal. She briefly introduced me as a sommelier to the general manager. Upon her introduction, I felt more like myself than I had my whole time in New York. She asked if we could talk outside, and I readily agreed. When she asked me to walk with her for a little I was slightly confused as to what was going on, but I wasn't going to question anything.

As I was about to comment on something like the weather, Danielle abruptly stopped. She told me she wanted to do something for me. Those had been Jeff's words months earlier, and I was now wary of any "help" people wanted to provide. Danielle asked me if I wanted to take over her position as wine director of White Street. She asked me as if it weren't a monumental moment.

I was still processing the bomb that had gone off in front of me when she faced me head-on. She said I had something she rarely saw in people and that she wanted to give this opportunity to me. I had a million questions. She said she had to go back inside but gave me her number. She hugged me and told me to think about her offer. Watching her disappear back inside White Street, all I could do was start processing everything. I stood in the same place for at least ten minutes, trying to wrap my mind around all that had unfolded during the afternoon. I had met someone who genuinely seemed interested in what I had to say, I had experienced support for my wine journey in New York for the first time, and I was pretty sure I had just been offered a job as a wine director.

To go from an absolute zero in New York's eyes to possibly running a wine program was almost too sensational for even me to believe. I resolved to keep walking. I wasn't even going in the direction of my apartment, but I needed to walk. Thoughts flooded my mind, and I ended up going for three miles. The way I saw it, I could toil away at a thankless position at Maialino for months. I would maintain a safe, stable, and predictable job. However, something in my mind told me I didn't come all this way to play it safe. I texted Danielle in the very moment I made up my mind.

I told her, "Yes."

Wine Talk: Terroir

I first heard the term *Rutherford dust* when my coworkers at Inglenook talked to me about the Cabernet Sauvignon blend called Rubicon. Whenever anyone spoke of it, they mentioned the smell and taste of the famous dust. As usual, I was completely in the dark and wondered why a winemaker would put dust into wine. I came to find out they were all talking about *terroir*.

When a coworker defined the term, my mind was illuminated. From my coworker's definition, I learned *terroir* wasn't just the dirt where vineyards were grown; it was more about the heart of a vineyard. This was an entirely new perspective for me. I learned the Rutherford dust was a combination of the vineyard location, soil, how workers tended the vine, and every other surrounding influence. I started seeing terroir as something living and breathing in wine. It's amazing how a bit of dust opened the world of wine to me in unimaginable ways.

All in all, terroir is the soul of a wine. It's as elusive as it is romantic. Having a firm grasp on terroir can give you a window through which to see even more clearly into a wine. Much like understanding complicated people, learning to understand the complicated parts of wine can be just as rewarding.

What is *terroir*?

Terroir is a French term, and it doesn't even have a direct translation into English. It's pronounced "ter-'wah." You can give the word an especially French-sounding pronunciation to seem even more in the know. The word seems somewhat mysterious or allusive.

Many people think it has to do with just soil types or the weather affecting the vines. These two influences are a part of terroir, but there is so much more to it. It is anything and everything that can impact how a vine grows and the kind of fruit it bears. Terroir takes into account macro elements like climate, soil, vine training systems, vineyard elevation, rainfall, average temperatures during the growing season, vine spacing, and the vineyard's orientation, or in which direction one chooses to plant a vineyard.

Terroir is all about the micro details too. Aspect, or how the sun hits a vineyard, wind impact, surrounding vegetation, any animals or insects coming into contact with the vine, any minor decisions a vineyard manager can make, and even the impact of the people living around the vineyard are all contributors to terroir. Tying together all these factors creates the terroir of a vineyard.

When wine experts go on and on about terroir, they are expressing what makes a particular wine so unique. If one can taste the terroir in a glass of wine, that's an accomplishment on behalf of the winemaker. For instance, if one is tasting a glass of wine from Champagne, there is a distinctive sense of terroir one can identify. Ideally, one will take in the sight of thin, persistent bubbles, smells of brioche and chalk, and the rich, refreshing mouthfeel on the palate and link them to terroir. By being able to do that for a glass of wine, the seemingly abstract nature of terroir becomes concrete. It's because one can actually smell the minerality coming from vines grown in the limestone soils, feel the electricity of acid from grapes ripened over the long, cool growing season, and sense the layers of flavor coming from Champagne's traditional method of production.

How can terroir be quantified?

We can look to certain aspects to try to explain why a wine is the way it is. There are ways to quantify the aromas, dryness, acid, alcohol, and body of a wine. However, there is no exact measurement of terroir.

Wine can be scientific and complex, but I consider terroir the essence a wine gives off based on the myriad of potential vineyard effectors. In terms of actually being able to measure terroir, it's just not possible.

Does wine always reflect terroir?

The answer is, unfortunately, no. Some wines are made from grapes grown in vineyards where terroir isn't the main concern. For bulk wines and larger vineyards, producers don't necessarily emphasize the specific terroir aspects. Vineyards like this lack many of the nuances and special attributes that reflect more terroir.

To make up for the lack of terroir in their vineyards, bulk wine producers do certain things to manipulate the finished wines. They can heavily irrigate to promote more grape production, let the grapes ripen longer to acquire higher sugar levels, and harvest high yields from vines. By doing these things, their resulting wines are more generic tasting and can't express a specific terroir of the vineyard. So, when you find a wine with the taste of its origins and tells a story of its terroir, savor every sip.

What are some examples of vineyards with famous terroir?

When I think of famous vineyards, France is the first place to pop into my mind. France has such a long history of honoring and preserving terroir in their wines. The most expensive bottles coming out of France are from Burgundy. Domaine de la Romanée-Conti is at the forefront of iconic producers and expensive wines. They own a particular vineyard called Romanée-Conti.

The vineyard is roughly four acres in size. The certain terroir elements leading to its distinction include rich limestone soils, fifty-year-old vines, small wine production, and a high reverence shown toward their vines. The vineyards are cultivated using only horses, and fewer than four hundred cases of wine are produced annually. A single bottle from this vineyard can sell for thousands of dollars.

Terroir isn't a term reserved for France. California has many vineyards showcasing distinctive terroir as well. The French may not want to hear this, but the truth is in the wine.

The Eisele Vineyard produces some the best Cabernet Sauvignon in the whole Napa Valley. The vineyard is just under forty acres in size and located in the northeastern part of Napa in Calistoga. The terroir the vineyard showcases is produced by its alluvial, stony soil and gentle slopes. The Eisele vineyard is protected from cool northern breezes by the Palisades mountain range. Those elements, combined with low-yielding vines and good drainage of the soil, all come together to create a one-of-a-kind terroir. The resulting wines are highly sought after and respected. Bottles of wine from this vineyard can sell for three hundred to four hundred dollars.

Wines with world-class terroir fetch lofty price tags. When you have a vineyard with an unmistakable character and terroir, the price can and does reflect it.

Can you actually taste the soil in wine?

Soil makes a huge difference in how grapes ripen and grow. The term *minerality* puts into words the effect soil and climate have on a finished wine. There is a debate among wine people about "tasting" soil in wine.

One school of people believes you can actually taste the soil in a wine. For instance, with a Riesling from Mosel, the slate minerality in the wine comes from the fact that the grapes are grown in blue Devonian slate soil. They believe the actual smells of the soil integrate into the grapes and into the finished wine.

However, the other school of people believes certain flavors in wine can come about as a result of the growing process. They believe the soil changes how grapes grow, and that's where the flavors come from, rather than the aromatic profile of the soil itself.

Another way to put it is the first school of people believes drinking Mosel Riesling is literally like licking slate soil, while the second school believes the essence of the slate appears in the wine because of how the grapes ripen in the distinctive soil. I happen to agree with the second school of thought.

I take a more holistic view when it comes to how grapes are grown. I believe how a vine interacts with its environment on a multitude of levels determines the final character of a wine. The struggle of the roots to find water, the elevation of the vineyard, the aspect, the weather conditions throughout the growing season, the character of the soil—I look to the interaction of all these elements to give wine its final character. There is so much more to a vine than the just the dirt it's grown in. Regardless of what team you are on, the link between soil, environment, and wine style is unbreakable.

13

Tables Do Turn

I SAID GOODBYE TO MAIALINO after only a month there. I felt that giving two weeks' notice was enough, especially after how I had been treated. I called Jeff to let him know. I needed to tell him why I was moving on. I felt like he needed to know how Kathy made me feel. When I told him over the phone about our conversation, he didn't believe me and assured me I had misunderstood her. As soon as he said those things, I knew my departure was more than necessary.

I spent the next two weeks answering questions about my new position with White Street. Many Maialino people were a mix of shocked and indifferent, and a select few were actually happy for me. Kathy and I never spoke again. On my last day, I walked out with my head held high. I survived my first hellish New York job. I had no regrets. The job got me to the city, and I had to go about trying to make it here.

With Maialino behind me, it was all White Street all the time. Danielle agreed to stay on for another month before starting her new job and assured me she wouldn't abandon me in the new position. I exuded confidence, but deep down being a wine director in New York scared the shit out of me. Whether I was scared or not, being able to work with wine every day brought me back the passion Maialino had been slowly draining me of.

Danielle introduced me to literally everyone I needed to know to survive in the New York wine industry. She made me feel like I could do it. It was as if I had a shot at being somebody there.

I didn't want to look like a wounded bird she was teaching how to fly, so on one of my first nights, I called in the only favor I had in New York. Marc from the whirlwind Corkbuzz night still kept in touch. He was curious about where I was working and wanted to support me. I could use all the support I could get, and I selfishly knew he and his friends had deep wallets. It was close to the time when Danielle would take off for her new position in wine distribution. Then I would be the one and only wine director and floor manager. Part of me just wanted to make sure she knew she'd made the right choice with me. I wanted to make her proud, and I called the men in for a visit.

Now, one thing I was oblivious to was just how slow it could be at the restaurant. When my gaggle of Goldman Sachs men arrived, they outwardly wondered why no one was eating there. Whether or not we were packed, the men came to drink, and that's all that mattered to me. I felt a rush of importance as the distinguished group gathered at the bar. Marc came over to Danielle and me, standing at the sommelier station, and pulled me close by the small of my waist. He kissed both checks, and I took it all in. He whispered in my ear to go grab them an expensive bottle. He said dealer's choice and to just surprise them.

Now that's what I envisioned in New York—the glamour, the thrill, the sexiness of it all. As I drank in the moment, Danielle asked what I was going to choose. Right, that was quite important. I threw caution to the wind, scaled the ladder in the cellar, and reached for a $3,500 bottle of 2010 Harlan Estate Cabernet Sauvignon from Napa Valley. As I descended the cellar ladder, I could feel everyone's eyes on me. I brought the bottle to the sommelier station to open it. I poured Danielle and myself a taste first. The rich, full, elegant wine filled my palate, and I thought, *This is what big money can buy on a Tuesday night.*

I prepared them with the finest glasses and poured the most expensive wine I had ever held. I made sure not to shake. They were pleased enough, and I spent an hour entertaining them, and they were generous with the pour they insisted I enjoy. When the check came, Marc threw down a card and didn't even look at the price. He left a more than generous tip, and just like that, they were off to the next extravagant event. He turned back and winked at me on his way out the door. I turned to Danielle, who was taken aback by the events that had just unfolded.

All she could say was, "Who are you?"

I smiled and thought to myself, *I'm a sommelier in New York City.*

For the next few months I was living my dream, but the dream was by no means tranquil. I was actually living a crash course in wine and restaurants. The responsibility and duties overwhelmed me at times, but I never put my gloves down, and kept on punching. I can honestly say I never imagined I would be responsible for dealing with a bartender who drank throughout a shift out of a coffee cup. I certainly didn't expect to work alongside a general manager who was the epitome of the shady "old" New York restaurant mentality.

Another curveball thrown my way was an employee who wore sleeveless outfits with unshaved and pungent armpits. It was somehow my responsibility to let her know of the customers' and fellow employees' grievances. There was no way for me to make our conversation about adopting deodorant and sleeves not awkward. On top of that, we didn't have consistent tables, I had more managerial issues than wine activities, and handling all the tedious background paperwork slowly killed me. Still, these realities didn't hold a candle to the soul-sucking effect of Maialino.

Despite the stress, strange situations, and colorful cast of coworkers, I felt important. I helped people choose and enjoy their wines. I was practically dancing around the restaurant and bringing people what I saw as joy. During my time of work fulfillment, I began to shift my mindset toward the city. Wine education and study were still my focus, but I realized I needed to engage in "the scene" of New York a bit, if for nothing else than to get my name out there and meet more wine people. Maybe instead of trying to hide from what I saw as the danger of New York, I should engage it. I had made a few friends here and there, but I also saw friends as a distraction and couldn't allow myself to get close to anyone.

I started to see life in New York as a "what do I have to lose?" situation. A couple of months after Danielle moved on to work for Whispering Angel, a Provence rosé brand, she offered me a social opportunity to exercise my new mentality. If you've never heard of Whispering Angel, it is known in some sommelier circles as a wine for the masses. Essentially, if a place sells wine, Whispering Angel is there. Not only that, they are also known to throw parties unlike anyone else. They wanted to create a desirable lifestyle intertwined with their wine. I found out firsthand about these outlandish affairs when Danielle invited me to a fashion event and said to bring a friend. There would be free-flowing drinks all night, and she insisted it would be a fun time.

Although not knowing what to expect, I agreed. In a way, I told New York City to let the games begin.

I arrived at the International Photography Center in what I considered my most stylish dress to dive into the high-end social scene of New York. There was a small-scale red carpet set up with cameras flashing. I couldn't help but feel the rush of it, even though I knew they could not have cared less who I was.

My friend Edisa was visibly shocked by the whole thing as well. After taking in the entrance and flashing bulbs, she and I made our way in to find Danielle. When I spotted her, Danielle was pouring out of a magnum of Whispering Angel surrounded by models and cameras. I got a glass and assumed my role as happy-go-lucky sommelier. I quickly shook off the feeling of inferiority and used my height and fearlessness to ingratiate myself with the partygoers. For all they knew, I was one of them. God, what a foreign yet intoxicating feeling.

Danielle rendezvoused with Edisa and me at the end of the event. I thought since it was 11:00 p.m. she wanted to say goodbye. I came to find out the night was far from over. Danielle introduced me to her friend Wei, who was *the* girl to know in the New York wine world, as well as her boss Paul and other higher-ups at the powerhouse Whispering Angel. Paul was French and charming. She insisted we all needed more drinks and food. I had to oblige.

Our little group made its way to a famous late-night restaurant in Tribeca. At that point, Paul and I had cozied up to one another. The night brought out my almost long-forgotten college exuberance for life and willingness to let all inhibitions down. We drank martinis and ate delicious food, and I didn't have a care in the world. I was beginning to get used to the outlandishness that was now becoming my New York reality. The night ended with me making out in the back of a cab with Paul. Very New York of me.

When I changed my outlook on how I was going to go about living in the city, the floodgates opened. Marc invited me to a Dom Pérignon tasting at a place called New York Vintners, which I had never heard of. The tickets turned out to be $1,500 a pop, but I was going at all costs. I arrived at a wine-shop-looking venue, and a member of the staff guided me down to the cellar, three stories below the entrance. All the stairs were lined with candles. If their goal was to evoke sensuality, the charms worked on me.

We reached the main room with walls lined with bottles, and I found Marc. My jaw dropped. I thanked him profusely and he handed me a cocktail. Marc directed my attention to a vivacious gentleman entertaining the crowd. He told me the man was Shane and he owned all of it. My interest now piqued, we all sauntered into a hidden room filled with champagne and the finest seafood towers I had ever beheld.

Shane sat at the head of the table by me the whole night, and the flirtation commenced. The more the bubbles filled me up, the more I forgot about trying to direct all my attention to Marc. As the night went on, I considered New York Vintners my own personal heaven. Shane explained they did classes, events, and sold wine every day. He made sure to give me a card and told me to come in anytime.

I was high off the circumstances surrounding me and enamored with these interesting, albeit filthy rich, people. I ended my evening of washing down lobster with thousands of dollars of Dom Pérignon by insisting that Shane let someone saber a magnum of champagne. He agreed, and we found a birthday girl. He handed her a sabering knife and instructed her to slide it along the neck to strike the top of the bottle. She did as she was told, and the top exploded from the bottle. With the cheers and excitement from the group, I felt my New York awakening gaining steam.

I went from complete avoidance of the New York social scene to willing acceptance and then to thriving on the thrills. People were just different there. It's as though nothing was off limits. I got a taste for it, and I needed more.

Several days later, Shane invited me for drinks. The good thing about the circles I was ingratiating myself in was the wine was spectacular. We went to a high-end wine bar and polished off a bottle of champagne almost too easily. I could tell he had the potential to be a very important friend in the city.

As autumn in New York neared, my intuition told me White Street was in trouble. The guests weren't picking up in the fall as we'd expected. Danielle promised me time after time White Street wasn't going out of business, but I doubted her. My fears were confirmed at the end of September. The restaurant wasn't closing immediately, but the owners sat me down and said things weren't looking good. They never gave an exact date, but said they simply wanted to be transparent.

Obviously, we couldn't share the news with the rest of the staff. At that point, I was about five months into New York and feared having to make yet another life-altering job change. I was scared of what my family or the outside world would think.

I was faced with a decision: Do I stay aboard a sinking ship and wait for its closing to blindside me? Or do I jump ship and find my next opportunity? I fully knew how it would look to change jobs yet again, but I had to let the fear of outside judgment fall to the wayside. I hunted for the next way to use wine in the unpredictable, crazy city I now called home. I asked myself where I would want to work next. Another restaurant was an option. I could always try to look into retail or even distribution. I had gotten to see the diversity of wine profession options in New York. My mind kept fixating on one place—the place that had piqued my fascination months previously. The thought of working as a wine educator at New York Vintners consumed me and provided the next path wine could take me down. I texted Shane inquiring about any open roles with New York Vintners. He immediately replied with a resounding "Yes."

With my next job secured and two weeks' notice given to White Street, the winds of change only blew more furiously. I gave it my all to the end but needed to keep moving forward. The general manager, Joel, wasn't exactly thrilled with me. He couldn't understand why I would leave. I simply needed to remind him of what the owners had said. He may not have been happy with my leaving, but I knew it was right for me. I felt more for my coworkers, who were confused by my seemingly abrupt departure. I had given my word not to indicate any chance of a closure. Despite the drama swirling around my White Street exit, I gazed ahead at the prospect of being a part of New York Vintners.

I had every intention of sailing out of White Street like a ship in the night. I didn't want a rowdy last night with them and certainly intended to avoid ruffling any more feathers. However, when my last managerial shift ended, my coworkers and comanager insisted I pick a bottle and have some wine at the bar.

Well, I supposed one drink wasn't a crime. After the equivalent of a full bottle of sparkling wine, my inhibitions came crumbling down. It seemed a grand exit was precisely what I would get. I invited my hostess friend, Jazmine, to come in on her night off and have a drink too. By 11:00 p.m., there was a congregation at the bar of people on the clock, off the clock, and friends of friends.

I embraced every cheer and additional glass of wine. My next "great" idea came shortly after midnight; I had the sudden desire to saber a bottle of sparkling wine. It seemed to be my drunken guilty pleasure. I told the bartender Becky she had to do it and feel how sensational it was to whack off the neck of a bottle with a knife. A few of us went to a hidden room in the back of the restaurant, which acted as our sexy speakeasy. There was no better place for a dangerous act. I grabbed a knife and showed her the technique. She slid the knife up the neck of the bottle, and the top of the bottle flew off. I had the usual rush of endorphins, but I wasn't done yet. The only thing better than one sabering would be two, and with even more fanfare.

The speakeasy crew rejoined the rowdy group at the bar. By this time our closing manager wasn't in the mood for fun anymore. He demanded the party move. I can't lie and say I worried at all. The mentality of my last night gave me far too much impetus for bad behavior. I assured him we would all go to another bar after one last saber.

For the grand finale I grabbed Jazmine and threw the knife in her hand. In the main dining room, with people gazing on, she masterfully sabered bottle. The staff erupted, and I was content with my farewell to White Street.

I had flown into the next chapter of my New York life with my blood pumping. After my departure from White Street, I hadn't felt so free in my life. I wasn't hurting anyone; I was just living on what I considered the edge. As a twenty-four-year-old woman in the most exciting city in the world, I would have regretted holding anything back. A particular quote became my battle cry, "It's better to be absolutely ridiculous, rather than absolutely boring." I promised myself to never let boredom render me docile.

The beauty of wine was its sheer ability to mirror my life. With wine, there was a time to study the history, geography, science, and proper service. Subsequently, there was a time to just knock a few glasses back. And then there is balance. I've always deeply appreciated balance in wine. To me, it seems fitting one's own life should have the same balance. New York let me indulge in the more outrageous side of life. I can't regret any of it because of that.

Wine Talk: Is Age Just a Number?

The oldest wine I had tried up until living in Napa had been a couple of years old. I simply never knew wines could age gracefully and transform. My whole tune changed the day I decided to visit an Inglenook coworker who had broken his foot and wasn't able to work for a few months.

I could tell he was lonely and simply needed someone to sit with him for an afternoon and lift his spirits. He lived about an hour and a half from Napa, but on one of my days off I made the drive south to visit him. As my coworker ushered me into his home, I realized he was an even greater wine aficionado than I'd thought. He took me on a tour of his handcrafted cellar. He had over five hundred bottles and pristine conditions to age each one seamlessly. His tour and wine cellar inspired me to ask countless questions. I needed to know what made wine age, how to do it, and any other details that could illuminate the unfamiliar practice to me.

After he fielded each question, he told me it was better to experience aged wine rather than to just talk about it. He asked me what year I was born, then disappeared into the cellar. Next thing I knew, he was carefully opening a bottle of 1991 Rubicon for us. As we sipped the over twenty-year-old wine, I was enamored with the color, smells, and feel of the wine. He took great pride in explaining to me why the color had turned to garnet, why the nose had dried fruits versus fresh, and why the wine tasted so smooth and mellow.

My unexpected crash course on aged wine expanded my appreciation for older bottles. It's in knowing the how, why, and what to expect from older bottles that makes the whole process more pleasurable. Maybe one day you can open another's eyes to the majesty of wine aged over twenty years, hopefully without a broken foot being involved!

Why do people age wine?

People age wine because certain wines can chemically change and become more interesting, complex, or integrated. Those may seem like a bunch of fancy words, but they mean the wine has a noticeable change in style over time and can become more fully developed. For me, the best way to compare old wine to younger wine is to think about wine in terms of seasons. A young wine is like spring, and an older wine is like fall.

When we think of spring we think of freshness, flowers just blooming, and perfume-like aromas filling the air from new plant life. Whether white or red, young wines have a bright, crisp nature. The aromas you smell in the wines are more primary, meaning the smells and flavors of the wine are dominated by fresh fruits. In addition, the aromas are somewhat one dimensional, and what you see is what you get with younger wines.

The word *autumn* evokes images of leaves changing color and falling from the trees. People typically think of warmth and spice. One can observe more depth and development in the season overall. Older wines experience a similar sensation, with the fruits turning more dried and more developed aromas and flavors appearing. Interestingly enough, older wines start to lose pigmentation and shift from vibrant ruby to more faded and rustier tones, much like dried leaves.

The changes I outlined above happen because of the wine's subtle exposure to oxygen. It's all chemical. Corks have microscopic holes through which small amounts of oxygen penetrate over time. The reason aging wines are stored on their side is to ensure the wine is in contact with the cork. By doing this, there isn't a huge gap that would negatively speed up the oxygen exposure. Graceful and slow aging is always the best way to go. Overall, people age wine to witness its evolution in the bottle over time.

What does *vintage* mean?

Many people think that saying a wine is vintage always means the wine is old. However, *vintage* refers to the year in which the grapes of a wine were grown and harvested. To speak about a wine's vintage is to simply convey that the grapes in the wine come from a particular year. The reason the vintage is included on the bottle and discussed is to give the person drinking the wine an idea of what to expect.

For instance, 2011 in Napa was a year when it rained closer to harvest and was cooler in general. Comparing 2011 with 2012, that year had more consistent warmth and no rains during harvest. Thus, by looking at the label, you can get an idea of the kind of wine inside based on the weather conditions from the given year.

Trust me, I don't know every vintage characteristic from every year from every growing region. But if you know what kind of wine you like, a simple google search can help you decide between two vintages. There are many sources that talk about the weather conditions from particular years and the resulting styles of wine. Jancis Robison's website is always my go-to for vintage info: www.jancisrobinson.com.

How do I know how long to age a wine?

Among the many astute questions I would receive as a sommelier, one was always, How long do I age X kind of wine? I can always give an estimated guess. I can look into the producer and where the wine was produced and understand the composition of the grape. Then I can make a suggestion to either drink it now, age it for five years, or let it age for twenty-plus years.

For instance, a vibrant Sauvignon Blanc from New Zealand isn't meant for aging and is in the *drink now* category. On the other hand, a Cabernet Sauvignon from Stellenbosch in South Africa would do well with five years of age to soften a bit and integrate its flavors. On the far end of the spectrum, a high-quality wine from Bordeaux will be hitting its stride after twenty years in the bottle due to its intense and hardy structure when it's first bottled.

The twenty-plus-year answer is the least well received because no one wants to wait that long. You know what they say about good things and waiting. You could absolutely take my recommendation, but there is one other way to know definitively how long to age a wine.

Honestly, the best way to obtain an accurate aging range is to ask the source. For instance, you are gifted an expensive bottle of Napa Cabernet Sauvignon. You have the desire to drink it the night after you receive it, but something tells you this bottle is special and can perhaps go the wine-aging distance. I recommend calling the winery and asking them. Since they made the wine, they will have the best idea of how long you should lay the wine down before drinking it. Some wines can change so greatly that they warrant the quick phone call.

Wines with high acid and high sugar are great for aging. However, depending on where a wine is grown and how the grapes were treated when making the wine, more aging may be warranted. There are a few grape varieties from specific regions that have historically aged quite well. If you have never tasted "old" wine, I would start with some of these examples.

The first aged wine I tasted was Napa Cabernet Sauvignon. I tasted a 1991 Rubicon from Inglenook. I finally understood what all the fuss was about with aging wines. The wine still had structure, fruit, and balance. Yet it seemed as though it had a greater depth and unity, and it inspired more thought when I was drinking it.

Other wines capable of the exciting changes age can reveal are Nebbiolo from Barolo, Tempranillo from Rioja, Cabernet Sauvignon blends from Bordeaux, Pinot Noir from Burgundy, Syrah from the Rhône Valley, Riesling from Mosel, Chenin Blanc from the Loire Valley, and of course Champagne. These are some great wines to get you started on the journey to appreciating wines with age.

What are some of the oldest wines in the world?

The wines that can go the distance have proven to be wines with high amounts of acid and sugar. Alongside this category, fortified wines have huge aging potential. The reasons these wines gracefully sleep for potentially a hundred-plus years is because of their structure to begin with.

The two best examples of nearly indestructible wines are Tokaji and port. Tokaji hails from Hungary and is made in a unique way using the Furmint grape. The concentrated sugars of the Furmint grapes are added into the freshly pressed grapes. The resulting wine has high levels of sugar with high levels of acid to match. There are many famous photos of bottles of Tokaji in cellars that have been aging for over a hundred years. The bottles are covered in fuzzy black mold, while the golden juice inside is perfectly preserved.

Port is a wine directly linked to process, much like Tokaji. The main difference between port and other forms of dessert wine is that the wine is fortified (a spirit is added to the wine to stop fermentation and retain excess sugar). Due to the fortification process, port can elegantly stand the test of time because of its intense and sturdy nature.

14

Savor Every Sip

THOSE FIRST FOUR YEARS OF MY WINE life set the stage for my passion and wanderlust. I did essentially every job one could do with wine from coast to coast, but it was never just a job for me. I let wine take hold of my heart. It colored my life and became a part of me. With every closed chapter and subsequent new chapter, my deep connection to wine never faded away. I trekked across the country because of it, I marveled at Napa Valley because of it, I pursued a career because of it, I took on New York City because of it, I had an endless supply of experiences because of it, and I woke up every morning with a purpose because of it. In that regard, I could never stop loving what I do and who I am.

Because of who I became in my years with wine in Napa and New York City, I resolved to develop my own wine project. It seemed only fitting to start a wine business and share my passion in the place where it all started for me. Thus, I made one final drive back to Jacksonville, Florida.

I developed my business, Wine Inspired, in 2018 to bring wine education, tastings, and events to my hometown. Every enlightenment, struggle, and triumph with wine during my first few years became the basis for Wine Inspired. It's the truest expression of myself and my dreams.

In spending my life telling wine's story, it ended up crafting mine. I have faith my story will continue with each sip of wine and in all the moments between them. I can rest assured wine will expose me to foreign lands and cultures. I'm certain I will find ways to bring people joy with it. I can be safe in the knowledge that I will befriend remarkable people in its name.

It's in striving toward and savoring those kinds of moments that defines what being alive means to me. I have no doubt my future will be filled with wine's magic because I will never give up on bringing its magic to life.

I realize now my work with wine was only partly about discovering and teaching all its mysteries. In searching for answers in wine, I found out who I truly was with every glass. In sharing wine, I'm able to share myself in the most authentic way. I have come to find that when you show people who you are, it gives them permission to do the same. How miraculous it is to find a way into people's hearts and, in doing so, let them into yours.

Wine Talk: Debunking Wine Myths

In thinking about misconceptions swirling around wine, I realize I had to debunk my own most misleading myth in order to grow in the study of it. I thought wine had to be competitive, serious, and a way to show off superior knowledge. When first starting out at Inglenook, I carried these misleading thoughts with me constantly. It took a simple statement from a wise man to bust my own myth.

Harold was an older gentleman and the Château Ambassador for Inglenook. One particular afternoon, we were polishing glassware in the bistro. He could tell I was being hard on myself for not possessing enough knowledge about wine. I expressed to him that I felt as if I would never be able to keep up with the sommeliers around me. At that moment, he knew I was heading down the wrong path with wine.

He told me one simple thing: "It's just grape juice." He let me know the way I related to people and created experiences for them using wine was far more important than any vast amount of knowledge I could ever attain.

Just like that, my mind went back to what wine meant to me sitting at my parents' table. It had always been just grape juice. That's what made it so special. It was the moments it had the potential to create and the emotions it could evoke that made me fall in love with it. I stopped studying wine for me and started studying it to see what I could make it mean to other people.

Hopefully, your perspective on wine will continue to grow and evolve. By debunking a few major myths and being open to discovering deeper answers within wine, you will undoubtedly build a stronger foundation for its appreciation. In doing so, you can continue to craft your own sensational moments with wine. Most importantly, you can share them with others too.

White wine only goes with fish, and red wine only goes with meat.

It's the age-old standby when it comes to wine pairings. Yet the saying couldn't be farther from the truth. There is an endless amount of creativity you can put into food-and-wine pairings. Instead of making pairings so cut and dried, there are insider tips that can help craft a sensational food-and-wine experience.

Certain red wines can go with fish, and certain white wines can go with meat. The primary considerations to take into account when choosing a wine are the structure and character of a dish. Also, the flavors of the sauce accompanying the main protein is vital when thinking of what wine to choose to enjoy with the meal. When looking at a meal like this, it's easy to see how different aspects of a dish can sing with a variety of wines.

For instance, you are enjoying a thick mahi-mahi with a rich butter-and-herb sauce. One might automatically reach for a white wine, but there are more options to play with. A light and spicy red wine or rosé could be a lovely match. Some examples of a red to pair with this dish include a Gamay from Beaujolais, a Grenache from the southern Rhône region, or a Pinot Noir from Burgundy or Oregon. The thickness and weight of the fish will stand up to those wines. Also, the butter sauce and herbs will create cohesion and smoothness in the reds mentioned.

Let's say you're having Parmesan-encrusted pork chops another night. With this kind of meat, red wines typically jump to mind. However, this dish could be equally satisfying with a white. You could easily pair a Pinot Gris from Alsace, Viognier from California, or even Premier Cru Chablis (the Chardonnay grape) with this dish. All these white wines have enough body and richness to stand up to the heavier pork. Their flavors will also complement the dish. There is a certain savory quality to the whites I mentioned that will work nicely with the Parmesan.

Hopefully, you have gained the confidence to pull out a light, fruity red with your next salmon feast. I would be equally impressed if you reached for the white Burgundy when you are enjoying some roast pheasant. By looking at food-and-wine pairings from multiple angles and with an open mind, you can do lots of delicious experimenting. Jump into food-and-wine pairings fearlessly and you could create something wonderfully unexpected.

White wine always comes from white grapes, and red wine comes from red grapes.
It seems impossible a white wine could come from a red grape. However, there is a simple explanation for this seemingly unbelievable phenomenon. Visualize this: I squeeze a red grape between two fingers and a white grape between my other two fingers. What color do you think the juice is running down my hands? *It's clear!*

All juice of all grapes is clear, save for the rarest kinds of grapes, called *teinturier*. You may never come across this word again, but it's good to have in your wine reserves. The term *teinturier* refers to grapes with such pigmented skins the juice is automatically purple as soon as the grape is squeezed.

Most important to remember, the skins of red or white grapes are what cause the color changes in finished wines. I include white here because there are wines called "orange wines," which are made from the juice of white grapes fermented with the skins. The finished wine takes on a coppery hue. Thus, the name "orange wine."

Another great part of the potential of clear juice being obtained from red grapes is the option to make a white wine from red grapes. If you have ever had champagne called *blanc de noir*, you have tasted this principle in practice. The term *blanc de noir* translates to "white from red." Thus, the champagne was made from the juice of Pinot Noir grapes that was separated from its skins. The result is an entirely white wine made from a red grape.

Sweet wines are lower-quality wines as opposed to dry wines.
A lot of people beginning their wine journey denounce their past love for "sweet" wines. They see wines with sugar as being for novices and immature palates. The truth is residual sugar is not the enemy in poor-quality wine. The real enemy is the poor-quality grapes used to make the wine in the first place. Some producers simply use sugar to mask the poor quality of the grapes.

A great way to rid yourself of the misconception is to try a really high-quality wine from Germany or Austria with leftover sugar. My best suggestion is a Mosel Riesling. And make sure to ask a wine shop employee if the wine has some leftover or residual sugar. Also ask the same question to obtain a wine from Austria by the name Grüner Vetliner Smaragd. These two wines will knock your socks off with their beautiful integration of sugar while maintaining a refreshing acid.

If you want to take the experience to the next level, drink these wines alongside stinky, runny cheeses or very spicy foods. The wine will make the cheese taste better and cool down the spice of a Thai dish, for instance. The cheese or spicy foods will prove the wines' power to evolve for the better, but also to stand up to a wide range of foods. Be careful: you may become "sweet" wine's new advocate.

"Wine people" hold their glass in a way that is pretentious.
At first glance, "wine people" look like they are merely trying to exert superiority over the "non-wine" folks. However, there are explanations behind why they handle wine the way they do. I have learned there is typically a rhyme and reason to a lot of the mysterious wine activities.

For instance, all the wine people holding the glass by the stem—they don't dare touch the bowl of the glass. Although it may seem like useless decorum, the main reason is because our hands give off body heat. This body heat could potentially change the character of the wine through temperature change. So, rather being safe than sorry, people grab the stem and not the bowl.

Now, what's all that twirling about? Are they just trying to look superior? Well, not exactly. The main reason for all the swirling is to aerate the wine. *Aerate* means making sure as much air as possible hits the wine. When wine and lots of air meet, the wine starts waking up, in a sense. The rapid chemical change causes the wine to give off more aroma and loosen up on the palate. By doing this yourself, you could look "pretentious," but it's completely worth it.

I can't get a fantastic bottle of wine for less than fifty bucks.
One of the most damning mistakes someone can make in wine is believing more expensive wines are *always* better. Also, people tend to stay in their lane in regard to wine choices. They order and buy the same wine time after time. A lot of the price of wine is driven by demand and familiarity. So, a wine from an unknown place made from an unknown grape could be just as good as or better than the one-hundred-dollar Napa Cabernet Sauvignon everyone holds in such high esteem.

For instance, regions such as Sicily in Italy, the Canary Islands of Spain, the Finger Lakes in New York, Beaujolais in France, and the Douro Valley in Portugal all offer wines at better prices because they are less discovered. The beauty of these regions is that many people haven't tried their wines. These specific regions tend to focus more on indigenous grape varieties as opposed to international grape varieties, like Cabernet Sauvignon and Chardonnay.

Try a new region making a unique wine, and be kind to your wallet while you're at it. Branching out with wine can be a rewarding way to expand your mind and palate. Never be afraid to explore the unknown when it comes to wine. You won't be disappointed.

Glossary of Wine Terms

acid: the component of wine causing a mouthwatering sensation on the palate

aerate: the exposing of wine to air, thus breaking it down slightly, releasing aroma and flavor

aroma: the smells of a wine coming from the different chemical compounds found within each respective wine

balance: when all the elements of a wine are in harmony without any particular one standing out or overshadowing another

barrel: a vessel used to age wine, resulting in the incorporation of toasty spice flavors and subtle oxygenation to a wine

body: refers to the weight of a wine on the palate, which can be heavy, medium, or light

CMS: Court of Master Sommeliers

decant: transferring wine from the bottle into a new vessel in order to aerate it or remove the wine from sediment

finish: the length of time a wine lingers on the palate after it has been swallowed, which can be long (a minute of more), medium (more than thirty seconds), or short (less than fifteen seconds)

legs: the droplets of liquid on the side of a wine glass

natural wine: a wine made in a noninterventionist method from grapes grown without the use of chemicals

New-World wine: a wine made from grapes grown outside of Europe (e.g., in the US, South America, or Australia), resulting in a more generous style of wine

Old-World wine: a wine made from grapes grown in Europe, resulting in a particularly rustic style of wine

oxygenation: the incorporation of oxygen into wine, causing a softening of the wine's feel on the palate and a heightening of the aromas on the nose

residual sugar: leftover grape sugar not fermented out of a wine during fermentation

sediment: the solid particles formed from color and tannin falling out of a wine that has undergone aging

sommelier: a wine professional responsible for conveying wine knowledge to enhance a wine experience in a restaurant, wine shop, or educational setting

tannin: phenolic compounds found in the skin of grapes and inside barrels, which are transferred to a wine, creating a drying sensation on the palate

terroir: any and all factors influencing a vineyard's grape production

traditional method: the method to create a sparkling wine involving the deliberate fermentation of grape juice inside a wine bottle, capturing the carbon dioxide and alcohol inside as the result of fermentation

varietal: the name for a particular kind of grape in the *Vitis vinifera* family of grapes

vintage: the year in which grapes were ripened in a vineyard

wine: a fermented beverage made from the juice of grapes

wine faults: negative effects on a wine, with cork taint and oxidation being two common faults

WSET: Wine and Spirit Education Trust